# Clément Marot

## Twayne's World Authors Series

David O'Connell, Editor

*University of Illinois*

TWAS 751

CLEMENT MAROT
(1496–1544)
*Moroni, "Portrait d'homme"*
*Photograph courtesy of*
*Photographie Bulloz*

# Clément Marot

## By George Joseph

*Brandeis University*

*Twayne Publishers • Boston*

*Clément Marot*

George Joseph

Copyright © 1985 by G.K. Hall & Company
All Rights Reserved
Published by Twayne Publishers
A Division of G. K. Hall & Co.
A publishing subsidiary of ITT
70 Lincoln Street
Boston, Massachusetts 02111

Book Production by Elizabeth Todesco
Book Design by Barbara Anderson

Printed on permanent/durable acid-free
paper and bound in the United States of
America.

Library of Congress Cataloging in Publication Data

Joseph, George, 1944–
    Clément Marot.

    (Twayne's world authors series; TWAS 751)
    Bibliography: p. 152
    Includes index.
    1. Marot, Clément, 1495?–1544—
Criticism and interpretation.
    I. Title.  II. Series.
PQ1635.J58  1985      841'.3      84–22534
ISBN 0–8057–6600–6

269829

*To John Porter Houston*

# Contents

# About the Author

George Joseph received his undergraduate degree from Oberlin College and his graduate degrees from Indiana University. He is an assistant professor of French at Brandeis University and formerly taught at Yale University. He has written on Malherbe, Ronsard, and Marot, as well as on Wolof oral poetry.

# Preface

Clément Marot was a French poet who wrote from about 1513 until his death in 1544. He was Francis I's major court poet and participated in that first flowering of the Renaissance in France that gave us Fontainebleau, the castles of the Loire Valley, Rabelais, and the venerable French institutions that we know today as the Collège de France and the Bibliothèque Nationale. Marot made at least two major contributions to this movement. His psalm translations marked the beginning of modern French prosody. His epigrams, verse epistles, and rondeaux established a natural way of writing poetry that inspired La Fontaine, provoked the admiration of Voltaire, and foreshadowed the late nineteenth-century ideal of literature about nothing. The freedom and simplicity of Marot's style are congenial to the twentieth-century reader.

## Renaissance Categories
## Necessary for Modern Criticism

After ten years of teaching and studying Marot in various settings, I have chosen to write this book with close attention to internal logic and as yet unexplored interrelationships among the poems. I have adopted a rather lean prose style in my own commentary for two purposes. One is to allow the professor using this book to interpolate his or her own interpretative cast on the works according to a variety of aesthetic and imaginative perspectives, values, and insights. The other is to make possible a new kind of intensive commentary on the texts themselves.

I find texts that are heavy on romantic readings and light on substantive analysis unhelpful. I am aware of new currents of literary criticism in French and have tried to write this text so it would at least be congenial to these and allow them to interact with it. However, this book employs little of the critical vocabulary characteristic of these methods. It mainly seeks to establish new perspectives on Marot's style by a carefully considered mixture of historic analysis and modern critical vision. The point of keeping these two approaches in tension is to introduce a stylistic framework for further academic study. Without this dual vision, the framework remains elusive and hidden.

For this purpose, I have couched my conclusions in terms of Renaissance rhetorical categories and concepts of lyric genre, which call for a clear and concise theoretical discourse. These categories, which are at once simple and erudite, have proved extremely successful in the classroom and induced lively discussions at scholarly meetings.

What I hope makes this volume different from others is my effort to give the historical approach the fluidity the modern mind requires to engage in a fruitful dialogue with a Renaissance poet whose critical mentality in some aspects resonates with our own. Marot's own use of conventions is strikingly modern. Singularly enough, irony, distance, and other such devices in his poetry are not so much directed at persons but turn in on his own literary work. For this reason, only a fusion of modern critical analysis with a historical approach will reveal Marot's modernity without obscuring his difference from us. Scholars who can straddle the two methods will find that each is a guarantee against the excesses of the other. Both together restore the polyvalence of Marot's poetic voice, with its suggestive, sometimes unresolved contrasts and juxtapositions. Marot plays masterfully with opposites: comic-tragic, head-heart, high-low. Elsewhere he delights in hiding behind deliberate ambiguity.

## The 1538 Arrangement

This study is the first to be based on the editions that Marot published in 1538 with Dolet and then Gryphius. Scholars unanimously agree that these editions, identical in nearly every respect, were the last to be published under the author's supervision. I have also considered major poems outside the 1538 arrangement: three of Marot's coq-à-l'âne epistles, some of the eclogues, the psalm translations, and poems of major religious consequence. Since scholars have not studied the 1538 arrangement, conclusions I reach represent a first look at what is possible rather than definitive answers. More work needs to be done, beginning with a modern critical edition.

The 1538 arrangement—based on a variety of factors including genre, chronology, size, and stylistic level—reveals previously unsuspected relationships between poems that cause us to revise significantly the standard definitions of Marot's poetic genres. Marot creates a system of genres that presses at the boundaries of traditional rhetorical classifications into high, middle, and low styles. I find that Marot elaborates most often on the low style. Of the genres he introduced in French, the epigram, eclogue, and elegy traditionally belong to the low style, as do the verse epistle, the rondeau, and the satire which he brought to a kind of perfection.

Considering Marot's style in terms of a sophisticated and coherent system of low-style genres permits the reader to identify the writerly aspects of a poetry that is characterized so often as conversationally transparent. Taken together and compared with one another, Marot's poetic genres reveal each other's stylistic principles. In contrast to Boileau's desultory "Imitons de Marot l'élégant badinage" (Let us imitate Marot's elegant banter), I see an aesthetic of "art that hides art," which is the ideal of Cicero's *De Oratore* and found a Renaissance expression in the *sprezzatura* (nonchalance) of Castiglione's *Book of the Courtier*. At times there are clashes between high and low style in Marot's poetry. But rather than intellectual frivolity, these clashes imply a nonchalantly ironic distance from high-style pretension.

Marot's nonchalance also sheds light on his pre-Pléiade methods of imitation. Older scholarship recognizes that Marot, unlike the Pléiade, does not attempt "to speak Greek and Latin in French" by scattering pastiches of classical poetry throughout his verse. I believe that it is important to reaffirm this older scholarly perception, first of all because the older scholarship itself does not work out its implications and second, because recent scholarship has forgotten it. Furthermore, claims about Marot's uncertain grasp of the classics do not take Marot's method sufficiently into account. Rather than displaying his learnedness with references to specific lines, Marot attempts to re-create natural, unpretentious, French equivalents of classical poetry. (It is no accident that Marot's psalm translations appealed to Jean Calvin whose *Institution chrétienne* is the first example of so-called Cartesian French prose.)

Marot's method required, on the one hand, a total assimilation of classical authors and, on the other, a careful evaluation of comparable means of expression in French. He adapts Ovid, Martial, and even David to French, whereas Ronsard adapts French to Pindar and Horace. The medieval French conventions that decorate Marot's imitations seem inappropriate to modern scholars; these conventions, however, rendered the classics accessible to French readers much as the high-pitched roofs and towers of the Loire castles adjusted the sun-inspired architecture of the Italian country gentleman to the rainier climate of the French knight.

My rhetorical approach has often led me to go beyond merely establishing relationships between Marot's poetry and the writings of others. Without wishing to supplant previous scholarship that tracks down hidden allusions but rather to complement it, I most often emphasize the internal relations between parts of a poem. My summaries of individual poems are oriented to this end. For example, past scholarship shows that the "Deploration for Florimond Robertet" draws on popular Renaissance themes of evangelism. But we can better understand Marot's use of these themes if we place evangelistic passages in the context of the entire poem, where we find considerable authorial irony and doubt cast on those passages.

## Enrichment: Biography and the Internal Approach

Such internal analyses combined with a careful attention to historical and biographical detail have led me to redefine Marot's poetic vocation in terms of the relationship between his life and works. Marot's personal life is full of mystery and contradictions. He alternated between the glory of being France's first poet and the humiliation of prison and exile.

It is tempting to seek out hidden religious depth beneath the many-faceted charm of Marot's wit. G. Defaux, for example, finds in Marot's simplicity and stylistic liberty a Christian conception of poetry: a writer can be an instrument of the Holy Spirit, whose indwelling presence guarantees the meanings and effectiveness of the poetic word. Defaux considers Marot's psalms the logical outcome of this aesthetic because they signify a total surrender of the poet's skills to the Divine Logos.

Court politics, however, outweigh mystical theology in most of Marot's poetry. Thus, despite Marot's sincere pronouncements of a religious vocation, I find that his stylistic liberty in poems such as the "Epistle to Lyon Jamet" signifies the nonchalance of the courtier-poet more than the freedom of the Holy Spirit.

Marot's style is clearly linked to his political fortunes. His early poetry, which was written to win a place at court, tries to impress his prospective patrons through a display of Rhétoriqueur poetic techniques. Once he is secure in royal favor, he writes in the free, simple, and witty style for which he is famous, whether he is in or out of prison, ill or well. He abandons that style, however, when royal protection becomes uncertain, as in the epistle he wrote to succeed his father, and in the poetry that he wrote in exile in order to win new patronage. For example, during the second exile, Marot resorts to the strategies of his early life. But now neoclassical elevation was coming into fashion at court. Thus in the eclogue for the birth of the dauphin, Marot turned from his preferred free style in order to ingratiate himself with the protectors of the new high style, Catherine de Médicis and the future Henri II.

Furthermore, Marot's overtly religious poetry is most often written for immediate nonreligious goals, such as returning to France or winning a new patron. Even his psalm translations, artistically innovative and sensitive as they may be, were originally commissioned by Francis I and expanded with the hope of gaining Calvin's support. (These considerations of patronage aside, I find it tenuous to infer, as G. Defaux does, a divine logocentrism from Marot's translations rather than from his original works.) The political nature of Marot's poetry cannot be dismissed as a mere excuse or superficial fiction permitting the poet to address more serious matters.

Marot left full-scale religious writing to his patrons such as Marguerite. It is true that there are many religious allusions in his poems. They enter into his hierarchy of genres in complicated ways that I shall discuss in the course of this study. But it is doubtful that they constitute part of a systematic metaphor determining the characteristics of his style.

The transparent poetry that Marot wrote while enjoying court favor resists extraneous allusions to the Holy Spirit. Reading too much religious import into Marot's worldly writing misses the logical and rhetorical subtlety of this Renaissance poet and makes his work uncharacteristically heavy. It is better to leave the delicate silence of Marot's wit and humor undisturbed. If there is an aesthetic of the Holy Spirit in Marot's work, it is so diluted and indirect as to be of little religious significance.

Personally, I find Marot's death poetry to contain his most moving religious feeling. He probably was a deeply religious man. However, I believe that court poetry was his primary vocation and that he was a victim of changing political circumstances, in which his work took on new implications.

Marot supported the court as an institution, but he often found himself at odds with other factions, both inside and outside its confines. Thus, he is not what H. Guy calls a "courtier of the opposition," a member of the court who was secretly opposed to it. The political atmosphere in sixteenth-century France was quite volatile and what we today call the "establishment" was far from monolithic. Very often the court stood in splendid political, spiritual, and intellectual isolation above the parties of Parlement, the Sorbonne, and the courts of justice. Thus Marot freely read his scathing attack on the French system of justice to the king, but hesitated to publish it. Within the royal court itself, however, there were rival factions vying with one another for the king's favor. Scholars such as M. Jeanneret, C. Martineau-Génieys, and F. Yates have shown that the French court was attempting to create a new religious synthesis that would include reformers and conservative Roman Catholics.

I call this position "court evangelism" to emphasize its political as well as its religious dimensions. Although grounded in a mystical theology of the Holy Spirit, it was also inspired by a desire to control political events from the court's privileged position above all parties. Unfortunately, the logic of this belief forced the proponents of court evangelism into the uneasy political situation of being all things to all people and of identifying with everyone yet no one.

I count Marot among such court evangelists and consider the contradictory defenses that he wrote denying yet implying his sympathies with Lutheranism as such an attempt to be all things to all parties. My view, therefore, differs from both sides of the recent scholarly conflict concerning Marot's religion, that between M. Screech and C.A. Mayer. The former's preference for Marot's statements in sympathy with Luther does an injustice to Marot's denials of Luther. The latter's view of Marot as a precursor of secular, humanist moralism does not take sufficiently into account the truly religious sentiments of the poetry. I also differ from P. Leblanc, who is sensitive to Marot's piety but neglects his arrogance and ambitiousness.

Marot played politics with his religious idealism, and his fortunes varied with the effects of his strategies. There were days of glory when Francis I accepted the poet's noncommital defenses as part of a court policy to assimilate both progressive and conservative religious parties into a new synthesis. There were, however, darker moments when Francis was so frightened by the possible treasonous implications of French Lutheranism that the side of Marot's poetry implying a courtier's openness to Luther appeared seditious. Then, using the very contradictions and silences intended securely to establish Marot securely in the royal good graces, hostile parties at court could band together with legal, educational, and religious authorities to drive him away into lonely exile.

Whether he was in or out of favor, Marot always demanded the respect due to him as a poet. His humility and modesty have been overstated. In "L'Enfer," he boasts of his association with Apollo and the muses, as well as with the members of the court. In later life, he asks for royal support on the grounds of his potential to become another Homer or Virgil. In the great Ferrara epistle to the king, he puts himself on an equal footing with the king by showing himself accountable only to God. The latter stance, however, comes from the freedom and self-awareness of the Renaissance artist rather than from an aesthetic of the Holy Spirit.

Marot reflects the Italian Renaissance concept of the autonomous artist in contrast to the medieval craftsman. He maintains the distance of a poet, as well as of a court evangelist, from all theological labels. Not only does he change his style to suit new situations, but he steps back from his art, smiles at it, and mocks it with a confident grace and mastery.

Marot's poetry is significant and original because it creatively combines the art of the Renaissance courtier with that of the Renaissance poet. On the one hand, Marot refines the insolent pride of Italian Renaissance artists such as Benvenuto Cellini with the subtle nonchalance of the courtier. On the other, he draws on the prestige of the poet to avoid the pitfalls of court sychophancy. Although he protests against his fate in the great Ferrara epistle, he demonstrates his fidelity to the king. In poems written for less difficult circumstances, he uses wit and humor to express allegiance to a patron while asserting his own integrity. Thus, Marot treads a fine line between complicity and distance with regard to power as well as religion. His delicate balance between loyalty and independence leaves him uncompromised in a potentially servile art and assures him poetic immortality.

*La mort n'y mord*

I acknowledge with deepest appreciation the many persons who helped me with the preparation of this book. I thank G.K. Hall and the employees of the Feldberg Computer Center at Brandeis University for their responsive efficiency in times of trial. I also thank Aaron Katchen and Judith Irvine for helping with matters of detail, and Edward Kaplan, Richard Lansing, and Edward Engleberg for their suggestions concerning individual chapters. But I owe special debts of gratitude to Walter and Nancy Lob for their personal support, to Gail Stockholm for her editorial assistance, and to John Porter Houston for his kind guidance.

George Joseph

*Brandeis University*

# Chronology

1522–1524  The court travels between the Loire Valley, Île de France, and Lyon.

1523  Birth of Marguerite, daughter of Francis I.

1524  Birth of Ronsard. Death of Queen Claude, wife of Francis I.

1525  The court at Lyon. February 24, Battle of Pavia. Francis I taken prisoner. Death of the duke of Alençon, husband of Marguerite d'Angoulême.

1526  Marot imprisoned at Châtelet for having broken Lent. Death of Jean Marot, the poet's father. Liberation and return of Francis I from Spain. Francis I's two elder sons, Francis and Henry, taken as hostages. Marot composes "L'Enfer" ("Hell").

1527  Marot briefly imprisoned for having aided a prisoner to escape. Marot named *valet de chambre du roi*. Death of Machiavelli. Death of Florimond Robertet. Trial and execution of Jacques de Beaune, seigneur de Semblançay. Sack of Rome. Death of the connétable de Bourbon. Marguerite d'Angoulême marries Henry d'Albret, king of Navarre.

1528  Death of Albrecht Dürer. Publication of Castiglione's *Book of the Courtier*.

1529  Peace of Cambrai.

1530  Francis I founds the Collège de France. Francis I's two sons liberated. Francis I marries Eleanor, sister of Charles V.

1531  Marot is ill with the plague. Marguerite de Navarre's *Miroir de l'âme pécheresse*. Death of Louise de Savoie.

1532  *L'Adolescence clémentine*. Rabelais: *Pantagruel*.

1533  *La Suite de l'adolescence clémentine*. Birth of Montaigne. Henry, son of Francis I, marries Catherine de Médicis. Death of Ariosto. Francis I's pilgrimage to Laura's tomb.

1534  *Affaire des placards*. Marot flees and is condemned for heresy in absentia. Rabelais: *Gargantua*.

1535  Marot enters the service of Renée de France, duchess of Ferrara, daughter of Louis XII. *Concours des blasons*. Execution of Sir Thomas More, author of *Utopia*.

1536  Marot flees Ferrara. Goes to Venice, then returns to Lyon, France, where he abjures. Death of Erasmus. Calvin: *Institutio Christiana*. Charles V invades Provence. Death of the dauphin, Francis. François Sagon: "Coup d'essai."

1537  Marot encounters Sagon. "Epître de Frippelippes." Bonaventure des Périers: *Cymbalum Mundi*. Marriage of Madeleine of France to James V of Scotland.

1538  *Les Oeuvres de Clément Marot.* The truce of Nice and the meeting of Aigues-Mortes.

1539  "Eglogue au roi sous les noms de Pan & Robin."

1540  Death of Guillaume Budé. Benvenuto Cellini in France. Charles V enters Paris.

1541  Roffet publishes Marot's *Trente psaumes de David*.

1542  Marot flees to Geneva.

1543  First edition of *Cinquante psaumes en français*.

1544  Marot dies at Turin. Birth of Francis, son of Henry and Catherine de Médicis. Victory of François de Bourbon at Ceresole. Treaty of Crépy. Maurice Scève: *Délie*. Constantin edition of Marot's works.

1547  Marnef publishes the *Epigrammes de Clément Marot faites à l'imitation de Martial*.

# Chapter One
# Glory and Exile

## In the Shadow of Glory: Early Years

Marot was born in 1496 at Cahors in Quercy.[1] We know nothing of his mother except that she was a southern woman. His father, Jean Marot, was born in Normandy near Caen and returned north from Cahors in 1506 to become a court poet for Anne of Brittany, queen of France, wife of Louis XII. When Anne of Brittany died, Francis I, then the duke of Angoulême, took Jean Marot in as valet de chambre. The position carried with it a more or less steady income—depending on the ability of government bureaucrats to meet the budget—as well as food and lodging. It entailed no special responsibilities in itself, not even a regular presence in the prince's bed chamber. Jean Marot probably filled the role of intermittent scribe, secretary, and reader, as well as court poet.

We know relatively little about Marot's childhood. His affection and respect for his father pierces the veil of pastoral conventions in the "Eclogue to the King," where he movingly tells us how his father would teach him to sing late at night by lamplight.[2] A few disparaging remarks from the second *coq-à-l'âne* about oafish schoolmasters who ruined his youth are all we know about his formal education. Even there, however, it is difficult to separate truth from satirical polemics. Marot may be simply repeating widely current denunciations (compare Rabelais, Erasmus) of the numerous collèges in the Parisian Latin Quarter. Jean de Boysonné's claim that Marot knew no Latin also seems a polemic exaggeration. Marot probably knew Latin but not as well as humanists such as Erasmus, Budé, or Dolet.

Although Marot's classical background was relatively weak, he was strong in the French tradition of his fathers. He implies that a significant part of his education was carried on informally in the shadow of the king's retinue through the repeated thanks he gives to the French court, his *maîtresse d'école* (schoolmistress), for refining his language. It was at the French court that Marot became well

1

acquainted with the *Romance of the Rose,* Villon, and Rhétoriqueurs
such as Chartier, Molinet, Crétin. Here he encountered Jean
Lemaire de Belges to whom he felt a special indebtedness.

In 1514 Marot's father placed him as a page to Nicolas de
Neufville, Francis I's secretary of finance in the chancellery. De
Neufville was Marot's only patron outside the royal family, and it
is probably in the secretary's office that Marot met Lyon Jamet, a
young clerk of finances who was to become Marot's lifelong friend.
At the same time or shortly thereafter, Marot also spent time
learning the language of litigation (*la chicane*) at the law courts of
Paris, le Palais. During this training period Marot belonged to
the *basoche,* an association of young law clerks also called the
"Enfans sans souci," who were known for their exploits in Parisian
taverns and cabarets such as the Pomme de Pin or the Lamproie.
The *basoche* put on satirical plays and maintained many colorful
traditions such as the annual planting of a tree from the forest of
Saint-Germain in the May Courtyard of the Palais. Marot celebrates
their joyous life, their traditions, and their actors such as Jean
Serre and Jean du Pontalais in various short poems. Later, around
1540, he wrote an epistle to the king on behalf of the *basoche*
(*Epîtres,* LIV) to plead for the group's privileges in face of growing
royal anger and impatience.

Marot also wrote poems in hopes of gaining royal patronage.
These included the then fashionable "formes fixes"—rondeaux,
ballades, and chants royaux—inherited from the Rhétoriqueurs,
two verse epistles, and a series of longer translations from Latin
and Greek. Marot presented one of these translations, the
"Judgment of Minos," to the newly crowned Francis I. A dialogue
between the three great captains of antiquity, Alexander, Scipio,
and Hannibal, it was meant to please the military-minded king.
Indeed, shortly after the coronation, Francis I and his jovial,
energetic entourage set out to conquer the Duchy of Milan, which
France had lost in 1513. The campaign culminated in the famous
Battle of Marignano, which brought Milan back into French hands
and rekindled French hopes for a presence in the Italian peninsula.
The reign was beginning well. Francis I's favorable reception of
the poem encouraged Marot to present him with "Le Temple de
Cupidon" ("The Temple of Cupid"), a long allegorical poem about
love.

## Road to Glory:
## The Retinue of Marguerite d'Alençon

The result of Marot's efforts was a recommendation to Francis I's sister, who gave him the position of valet de chambre. Marguerite was a very powerful woman, who worked closely with her brother and her mother, Louise de Savoie, to make the royal court a brilliant and polished center of culture. She often assumed the responsibilities of Francis's queen, the retiring, deformed Claude de France. Marguerite was also an author herself (e.g., *L'Heptameron*) and an active patroness of the arts and letters. Among others, Rabelais, Héroet, and Scève could count on her protection. Marot, however, along with Victor Brodeau, was the first poet Marguerite had taken in.

**Court evangelism.**   Marguerite was also one of the major forces behind the rise of Neoplatonism in France and encouraged the reform movements that were beginning to take place in the church. Especially to her liking were the mystical tendencies of Lefèvre d'Etaples and Guillaume Briçonnet, bishop of Meaux. The latter, who turned his diocese into a center for evangelism, became Marguerite's director of conscience. In swollen, emphatic letters to her, he often attempted to guide her to heights of mystical contemplation. This circle of reformers, often called the Meaux evangelists, constituted an independent reform movement in its own right. It followed Luther with interest and criticized Rome. But under Marguerite's protection, it remained a nonschismatic court evangelism that tried to remain above religious parties.

**A witness to moral truths.**   We have very little specific information on Marot's activities at Marguerite's court. He was definitely a court poet and a secretary to whom she dictated her letters and other writings. In 1520 Marot accompanied Marguerite to the fabulous Camp of the Cloth of Gold, where Francis I met England's Henry VIII with the vain hope of creating an alliance against Charles V. For a full week, the two young monarchs, still in their twenties, vied to outdo each other in feasts and tournaments. Such was the lavishness of the affair that Martin du Bellay said in his *Mémoires* that the French nobility had sold its forests, mills, and fields to wear them on its back.

Marot, however, abstains from describing this dazzling splendor in the rondeau and ballade he wrote for the occasion (O.D., XXX and LXXIV). Rather he emphasizes moral categories as if to call the reader to see beyond flashy appearances and judge the meeting in terms of its success in bringing about peace and harmony.

In June 1521, Marot accompanied the duke of Alençon, Marguerite's husband, on a military expedition in Hainaut over the frontier from Champagne to stave off the forces of the Hapsburg Holy Roman Emperor Charles V. The duke of Alençon, no military genius, was named head of the expedition, probably out of deference to Marguerite. Francis I arrived on the field in October to take charge personally. Finally, on October 22, he obliged the imperial troops to retreat but mistakenly decided not to pursue his enemy. Never again would he have the opportunity to defeat his enemy so roundly.

Marot's mission was most likely to keep Marguerite informed of her husband's activities. The five pieces he wrote for the occasion range from lusty optimism before the battle to a longing for peace once the horrors of war had become apparent.[3] This evolution saves Marot's praises of the duke from being mere rhetorical flattery.

We know virtually nothing about Marot between the years 1522 and 1525. Formerly it was thought that Marot accompanied Francis I to the Battle of Pavia in 1525 because his first elegy is written by a soldier wounded and taken prisoner. We now realize that it is a mistake to confuse the narrator of the poem with Marot. During this disastrous battle—a sort of anti-Marignano that lost Milan and put an end to French aspirations in Italy—Francis I himself was taken prisoner to Madrid along with many of his men-in-arms and retinue.

It would seem that Marot remained behind with the court in Lyon. The poems he wrote for the woman intellectual from Lyon, Jeanne Gaillarde, suggest this. Marot also wrote epitaphs for various court personages and several love poems. Critics have long ago given up trying to identify the object of Marot's affections in the latter.

**A court evangelist imprisoned for Lutheranism.** The next we hear of Marot is in 1526 when he was imprisoned in Châtelet, which at the time housed the civil and criminal courts and prisons for Paris. The traditional story comes mostly from Marot's poems themselves. A woman, Isabeau, whom the poet had denounced for infidelity in a poem (probably O.D., LXIII), turned him in for having eaten meat during Lent.

In an attempt to gain his freedom, Marot first addressed an epistle to a certain Bouchard, doctor of theology (*Epîtres*, IX). (Bouchard's true identity and the precise authority he held is unclear.) Then Marot wrote the famous epistle to his friend Lyon Jamet, whom he met while a law clerk (*Epîtres*, X). Thanks to Lyon, Marot was transferred to Chartres by the bishop Louis Guillard, where he was held in an inn called L'Aigle. While there he wrote "L'Enfer" ("Hell"), his famous satire on lawyers and justice. He may also have been putting the finishing touches on an edition of the *Romance of the Rose* which was published later in 1526.

It is doubtful whether Marot had actually been denounced by his mistress, whom he calls Luna ("Changeful") in "Hell." The legend to that effect that he cultivates in his poetry seems more an echo of Villon's *Lais* and *Testament* than actual historical fact. For Villon, too, accused his mistress for having denounced him.

There also exists some controversy as to whether the poet was imprisoned for having broken Lent. Most critics have assumed that Marot did so, on the basis of the expression *manger le lard* (eat the pork fat), which occurs in a ballade written against his friend (O.D., LXXX) and elsewhere. This expression is a proverb which means "to be guilty of theft," and some scholars maintain that it is a mistake to understand it literally. Yet such an argument overlooks the playful tendency Marot inherited from the Rhétoriqueurs to reactivate literal meanings of figurative expressions.

In any case, all agree that Marot was imprisoned for some deviation from papal orthodoxy. His fate was the result of a strong Catholic reaction to heresy which had been brewing since 1524, when a preacher, Aimé Meigret, delivered a series of sermons in Lyon and Grenoble in defense of Luther and in condemnation of the church's commandment to abstinence. In 1526, with Francis I in captivity, the Sorbonne in conjunction with the Parlement had untrammeled power to act. Armed with papal orders and the approval of Louise de Savoie—now regent—it pursued all departures from strict orthodoxy as signs of Lutheranism. Marguerite's circle was as open to attack as any other, especially because Marguerite had to negotiate in Spain for her brother's release. Briçonnet, Lefèvre d'Etaples, and many others were subject to arrest. They were saved at the last minute by the regent or by Marguerite when she was not in Spain. This race between members of the court and the Parlement reveals that the French government was not at all unified. The court was an independent force often at odds with its own laws and procedure.

As it was in government, so it was in religion. The French court, as we have mentioned, had a legitimate claim to be an agent of reform within the church and above religious parties. Indeed, the original meaning of *reform* in religion referred to a noble person's reorganization of a monastery or convent. The need for reform was almost universally felt—one has only to read the histories of Renaudet or Imbart de la Tour to learn of the widespread corruption. In such a time, people turned to their rulers for reform both of doctrine and of the clergy itself.

We believe that Marot was a court evangelist who counted on the monarchy as the final source of religious and judicial recourse. In his epistle addressed to a theologian, Bouchard, and in his famous satire "Hell," addressed to the judges of Châtelet, he flippantly denies all party labels, protests his orthodoxy in simple terms, and asserts the power of his "friends" at court to free him. Such a defense constitutes a flat refusal so much as to discuss matters with religious and judicial authorities on the basis of the poet's royal connections.

Marot's liberation came indeed from the court. Only after Francis I returned from captivity in Spain was Marot released by order of the king. The poet celebrates his liberation in a joyous rondeau (O.D., LXIV), but the scars remained. He castigates Isabeau later in the first coq-à-l'âne, various epigrams, and perhaps one of the songs (O.L., XXIV).

The year 1527 marks the close of this period in Marot's life. Marot succeeded his father as one of Francis I's valets de chambre, and Marguerite, whose husband had died shortly after the Battle of Pavia, married Henri d'Albret, king of Navarre.

## Glory: Valet de Chambre to the King

Francis I held one of the most itinerant courts of the period, judging from the complaining letters foreign diplomats sent home to their governments. The king wandered—slowly, elegantly, and with a retinue of thousands—between Paris, Fontainebleau, and the castles of the Loire Valley. Even when he settled in one place, he would disappear to hunt in the forests, much to the consternation of ambassadors and others who had to go chasing after him. Francis I also undertook more extensive journeys throughout France, and during military campaigns in Italy, he settled the court in Lyon, which would become his wartime capital. Marot often may have remained behind in Paris—or Orleans, judging from his pieces dedicated to people from there.

It was at the courts of Francis I and Marguerite that Marot was first exposed to Italian influences. Francis I gathered a team of Italian writers and artists around him including Primaticcio, Cellini, Luigi Alamanni, Leonardo da Vinci, and Castiglione, who wrote his book on manners, the famous *Book of the Courtier,* at the behest of the French king. The king's country residence, Fontainebleau, was the center of this activity and in itself remains one of the Italians' most famous architectural and cultural achievements.

Semblançay.    Marot's new position seemed to increase his free spirit. The former *basochien* may have been involved in some antiestablishment prank when he helped to free a prisoner from the watch—although he denies the charge in the witty epistle he wrote asking the king to free him (*Epîtres,* XI). And in 1527 he bravely wrote two poems commemorating the hanging of Jacques de Beaune, seigneur de Semblançay, and Francis I's superintendent of finances, on charges of embezzlement.

Semblançay belonged to one of a few very powerful families who dominated the realm of high finance in sixteenth-century France. We remember them today for their châteaux, Chenonceaux and Azay-le-Rideau, but their power frightened the traditional French aristocracy, which owed its position to military prowess and came from an agrarian society. Semblançay seems to have been more of a victim of the clash of two worlds than of any true crime. His troubles began in 1522 at the defeat of LaBicocca. One reason for the loss was that the king's officers had not received enough money in time to pay their mercenaries. When asked why he had not sent the money, Semblançay answered that he had tried to take it from the queen mother's accounts, but that she had refused. This incident earned him the greedy Louise de Savoie's undying hatred, and it was through her efforts that he was finally hanged five years later. Public opinion was sharply divided over the event. Semblançay had been generous to many during his long, distinguished public career. Furthermore, Marguerite's correspondence reveals that she herself had been working on his behalf because he was Briçonnet's uncle. Many, therefore, mourned him, but others identified him with his class and felt his death to be a good example. Marot himself trod a fine line between the two points of view in both the epigram and the elegy he wrote on the subject.

**Florimond Robertet.** Marot's undaunted spirit comes yet again to the fore in the "Déploration de Florimond Robertet" ("Deploration for Florimond Robertet") (*O.L.,* VI), a poem he wrote for the death of the secretary of state in finances on 29 November 1527. The Robertet family, like that of Beaune, was one of the important families involved in high finance. Robertet at his death was one of four treasurers of France, a position second only to that of the unfortunate Semblançay. Florimond Robertet was also a great patron of the arts. He built the much regretted Château de Bury, ordered works by Michelangelo and da Vinci, and protected numerous men of letters including Marot and Budé. Marot's attacks in the poem on the lavishness of the church and monasticism belong to a long medieval tradition of anticlericalism. Notwithstanding, in the charged atmosphere of the early Reformation, they may have represented a political act of graver importance.

**Administrative difficulties.** At the end of 1527, the valet de chambre learned that he had not been inscribed on the rolls of the king's household (*couché en son état*) and was thus not due to receive the annual salary he was expecting. A careful poetic letter-writing campaign (see *Epîtres,* XII-XIV, and *Epig.,* XX) got Marot his wages, but having been burned once, he began another campaign to be inscribed in the king's household for the year 1528 (see *Epîtres,* XV and *Epig.,* XXI). This too was successful and marked the beginning of a period from 1528 to 1534 during which Marot basked in the sun of royal favor and popular acclaim.

## Pinnacle of Glory

As court poet, Marot wrote of events both large and small. On 11 March 1529, when the court left Paris for the Loire Valley, there appeared a poem falsely attributed to Marot that mockingly insulted prominent loose women of Paris, such as Jeanne Hénard, who was the wife of future chancellor Antoine du Bourg and who used all her feminine resources to gain her husband's advancement; and the famous "lingères du Palais," sewing women whose shop was a meeting place for all sorts and conditions of men in search of female companionship. Thus began the "Affaire des Dames." Marot defends himself in two poems (*O.S.,* II and III) where he takes a stand for a level of satire that does not descend to gross insult.

**France makes peace with the emperor.** Although Francis I had come home from Madrid in 1526, the consequences of his captivity did not end until the August 1529 Treaty of Cambrai (see *O.D.*, LVII), which had been negotiated by three women—Louise de Savoie, Marguerite, and Eleanor, sister of Charles V—along with Francis I's *grand maître,* Montmorency. The treaty stipulated that Francis I was to marry Eleanor and that Francis's two sons, whom he had had to deliver as hostages to win his own freedom, were to return to France. Marot wrote very little for the events that followed. A ballade presented at the king's levee announced the news of the royal children's liberation. An epistle of welcome to Eleanor and minor poems written to the Lorraine family who attended the wedding are all Marot wrote to celebrate Eleanor's arrival in France and her marriage and coronation.

**Misfortunes: Illness, theft, prison.** During the celebration, Marot—probably counting on royal largesse customary at such times—wrote an epigram requesting a little money. The king obliged, but Marot was not able to take advantage of the gift. First he fell ill with some version of the plague, which lasted throughout the winter of 1531–32. In the middle of his illness, Marot's valet, a man from Gascony, robbed him not only of his money but also of his horse and clothes. Thus in January 1532, Marot sent his famous verse epistle "To the King, on Having Been Robbed" (*Epîtres,* XXV). Francis I received the epistle favorably, and Marot wrote a short epistle (*Epîtres,* XXVI) to Jacques Colin to help him with the details of the money transfer. Epistle XXV generated the saying "faire le valet de Marot," which means "to steal," as well as several poetic replies including an unidentified attack on Marot for slander against Gascons. Marot wittily denies the charge in a verse epistle (*Epîtres,* XXVII) where he wonders whether his attacker is related to his thieving valet.

Marot's illness is probably the reason that his poetic production thins out during this period. Rumors were rife that Marot had died. Charles de Sainte-Marthe upon hearing the news exclaimed, "Then French poetry is dead!" Happily the rumors were unfounded. Marot was slowly recovering only to be arrested again for eating meat during Lent. Marguerite and her husband bailed him out.

**New genres, translations, and collected works.** Louise de Savoie died in 1531 during the same epidemic that had claimed Marot as victim. The poet wrote an eclogue (*O.L.,* LXXXVII) and an epitaph (*O.D.,* CIV). The former, the first eclogue to be written in French, is an example of Marot's innovation in the realm of poetic genre. Marot also wrote about this time the first coq-à-l'âne addressed to Lyon Jamet (I accept Guiffrey's chronology here), thereby creating another genre for French poetry. It is a satirical poem wherein Marot alludes to many current events including the Battle of Pavia, the bombardment of Florence, and his imprisonment. Both the eclogue and the coq-à-l'âne were immense successes. So great was Marot's popularity that he inspired imitators, detractors, and even forgers.

To defend himself against the false versions of his works, Marot published a collection of youthful works in 1532 with the editor Roffet. The title *Adolescence clémentine* comes from the Latin *adulescentia* which refers to the period of life from the fourteenth to the twenty-eighth year. Marot fudges a little. He includes poems he wrote up to his thirtieth year, 1526. In the preface, Marot presents these poems as a *coup d'essai*, a "tryout." Marot arranged the pieces both in chronological order and according to genre. Classifying according to genre is a Renaissance notion contrary to the tastes of the preceding period, which favored mixing. Thus here, as in the genres he introduced, Marot is an innovator in French. First come the early translations, and then the epistles, complaints and epitaphs, ballades, rondeaux, dizains, blasons, envoys, and finally the chansons. At the end of the volume is a section of works composed since "adolescence," including the deploration for Florimond Robertet, the eclogue for Louise de Savoie, the prison epistle to the king, the coq-à-l'âne, and works relating to Marot's illness. Having been recently arrested, however, Marot shows some discretion in poems he chose to omit from the edition. Notably absent are "Hell," and the epistles to Bouchard and Lyon. The book was one of the most popular of the period; it went through at least twenty-two editions between 1532 and 1538.

In September 1533, Marot published the first modern edition of Villon's works, entitled *Les Oeuvres de François Villon de Paris*. In the preface, Marot announces that he wants to reestablish and modernize a text that has become terribly corrupt. His notes to this edition are an extremely interesting attempt at philology.

Toward the end of 1533, Marot published a new collection of poetic works with Roffet's widow. The full title is *La Suite de l'adolescence clémentine, dont le contenu s'ensuit: Les Elégies de l'auteur, les epîtres différentes, les chants divers, le cimetière et le menu*. The liminary pieces announce that the book was published without Marot's knowledge. Yet, as C.A. Mayer observes, we have every reason to believe that Marot was indeed responsible for its publication because he never denied authorship.

Although Marot was at the height of his popularity during this period (1531–33), we know very little about his personal life. A fleeting allusion to his wife and children in a poem Louis de Centimaison wrote during the "Affaire des Dames" is one of the few references to his family life. Marot had two children, Michel and a daughter who became a nun under Marguerite's protection. Nothing is known about his wife. Earlier scholarship held that Marot had an affair with Anne d'Alençon, but such conjectures are now generally discredited. It also remains uncertain to what extent Marot traveled with the court.

**Religious rumblings.** Marot's popularity and position, however, were soon to prove fragile protection against the religious forces gaining momentum at the time. Tensions were high. Statues had been defaced, the Sorbonne mounted an attack on printing as a source of heresy, and Louis Berquin was burned at the stake despite the king's continued protection. This was a good example of the uncertainty of royal patronage in a world where the court and the bureaucracy often worked against each other. The sovereign was momentarily absent when Berquin was executed.

During Lent, 1533, Francis I set out on the first part of a great journey throughout all of France. He wished to introduce his new queen, Eleanor, and his son, the dauphin François, recently returned from captivity. The king and queen of Navarre remained behind at the Louvre, where Marguerite invited Gérard Roussel to preach for Lent. Roussel's sermons, filled with the evangelism of Lefèvre and so-called "bibliens," drew overflow audiences to the Louvre. The Sorbonne protested with a violent campaign against Roussel. Public order broke down, and there were sporadic riots in the streets. The king of Navarre was obliged to send to Francis I for help. The latter immediately exiled the leaders of the revolt from the Sorbonne, much to the embarrassment of its faculty and the glee of its students, who immediately began to cover the walls with placards deriding their professors. The Sorbonists replied in kind. Especially menacing was a scathing poem calling for the burning of Lutherans ("Au feu, au feu cette hérésie"). Marot courageously sent a reply to the walls with a rondeau ("En l'eau en l'eau . . .") condemning the Sorbonists to the water. The Sorbonne once again tried to convince the king to abolish printing—to no avail, thanks to the good influences of Budé and the bishop Guillaume du Bellay.

Marguerite had joined Francis I in Marseilles, where he was to meet Pope Clement VII to discuss the new heresies, when a vicious campaign against her was mounted in Paris, including an insulting play showing Marguerite under the influence of Moegera (Magister Gerardus). The publication created a scandal. The students and their principal were arrested. Then, in 1533, the Sorbonists condemned a second edition of Marguerite's *Miroir de l'âme pécheresse* for heresy. The work had been published two years earlier in 1531 without creating any reactions, and the case against it was thin. Unable to find any departure from doctrine, the Sorbonne condemned the book for heresy by omission—Marguerite had spoken neither of the saints nor of purgatory. The king was furious and wrote to the Sorbonne asking if the news of their recent condemnation was true and, if so, to please cite the specific passages they had in mind. The Sorbonne backed down—it is difficult to cite omissions—but continued its battle against religious and intellectual reform by now attacking the Collège des lecteurs royaux.

Francis I had founded this institution—the ancestor of the Collège de France—in 1530 as a foyer of humanist learning. (Education, like religion and justice was far from exhibiting massive uniformity in sixteenth-century France.) The Sorbonne remained attached to methods of scholasticism, and declared Latin, which it taught with medieval methods, as the only sacred language. The new Collège, on the other hand, emphasized a philological approach to biblical texts and based its studies on a sound knowledge of Greek and Hebrew as well as a renewed understanding of classical Latin. The Sorbonne's attack on this court-protected institution provoked the arrest of its own leaders.

Proponents of religious reform, including Marot, were much heartened by this turn of events. In the beginning of 1534, Marot published his translation of the first book of Ovid's *Metamorphoses* with Etienne Roffet and felt safe enough to include the principal works relating to his imprisonment—except "Hell." Of these, the epistle to Bouchard is the most interesting, for in this edition, Marot says that he is neither Lutheran, Zwinglian, nor papist. Later in 1538, he will change the word papist to Anabaptist.

Marot's confidence in a bright future for reform is also apparent in an epistle (*Epîtres,* XXXIII) he wrote for the marriage of Marguerite's sister-in-law Isabelle de Navarre with René de Rohan in August 1534. It was during this celebration that Marot had his first argument with François Sagon, whom he criticized for religious conservatism. The two men came to blows and had to be separated. Thus began their famous quarrel that was to flare up in verse a few years later in 1537.

## Exile

**The affaire des placards.** The king's favorable attitude toward evangelism suddenly ended on the night of October 17–18 when placards condemning the papal mass were posted throughout several cities and towns of France from Paris to Orléans. Such a fanatical act might well have gone unnoticed except that one of these tracts was posted on the door of the king's bedroom at Amboise while he was in residence. The father of the French Renaissance and hope of the reformers suddenly became a raging tyrant as he perceived a threat to royal authority possibly from members of his innermost circles. Francis abolished printing—a short-lived measure—and unleashed a wave of burnings and mutilations of anyone, regardless of social class, who was suspected of heresy. Many of the victims remained admirably steadfast, even as the flames leapt up about them. But others, including Marot, did not wait for such martyrdom. Marot fled to Marguerite, who was holding court at Nérac, but she could not keep him for long. She herself was suspect, and in January Marot was summoned with fifty-two other persons in a list that was published in the streets of Paris. His house had been searched and his books confiscated—books that condemned him in the eyes of his accusers because they included a translation of the Bible (a crime punishable by hanging), books on alchemy, and even perhaps some of the ignominious placards. Marguerite helped Marot on his way to Italy and the court of her cousin Renée de France. We believe it significant that Marot fled from one member of the royal family to another. His religion was that of the progressive members of the court; they had to wait in the hope that the king would join them again in their desire to work out a religious synthesis of all parties.

**Ferrara.** Once in Ferrara, Marot wrote his own letter of introduction in a verse epistle (*Epîtres,* XXXIV) addressed to Renée. The duchess took him on as a secretary along with other French refugees including Marot's friend Lyon Jamet. Renée's, however, was a divided household. Marot had celebrated her marriage in 1528 with the first epithalamium written in French. The marriage was to seal a Franco-Ferrarese alliance forever, but Renée's father-in-law had recently died, and her husband was in the throes of investiture negotiations with his overlords, the emperor and the pope. He no longer wanted to cultivate French ties, and in any case, he hated his wife. She was ugly and crippled, and her reformist sympathies—she would later convert to Calvinism—offended his zealously Catholic faith.

Renée, on the other hand, the daughter of France's Louis XII, considered herself to have deserved more than a petty duke in marriage. She had accepted her fate as a sacrifice to her country, but she never really took Marot's advice in his epithalamium to accept her new life. Rather she surrounded herself with a circle of French intimates. In fact, one of the conditions of the marriage was that she could take Michelle de Saubonne and the latter's daughters—Anne de Pons, Charlotte, and Renée de Parthenay—to Ferrara with her. When Anne of Brittany was on her deathbed, she entrusted Renée—then a mere child—to Saubonne. It was Saubonne, by the way, who had introduced Jean Marot to court. Now she was to help Marot the son.

Despite Renée's scorn, Ferrara under the Este was second only to Florence as a cultural center in Renaissance Italy. The Estes had patronized Boiardo, the author of *Orlando innamorato;* Ariosto had published *Orlando furioso* there; and Marot succeeded Bernardo Tasso, father of Torquato Tasso, as secretary. The scene of such endeavors was the elegant ducal castle and an island-garden, the Bosquet, on the Po. There Marot probably met the brilliant humanist Celio Calcagnini. With Calcagnini's help Marot improved his Latin. In particular, he read Ovid's *Tristia* and *Ex Ponto,* and the Latin satirical poets, Martial, Juvenal, and Persius. Under such tutelage, Marot learned that it was no longer fashionable to imitate the Petrarchan poets, whose influence is much less evident in his later work.

Marot also had occasion to meet French travelers passing through Ferrara. Notably, the cardinal Jean du Bellay with his doctor François Rabelais stopped on the way to Rome to pay his respects, and Jean Calvin, under the pseudonym Charles d'Espeville, came to seek refuge. Marot could hardly have found a better place of exile. Furthermore, it was a good time to be in Ferrara. The duke—to whom

Marot addressed a short epigram—left for Rome in September on a prolonged trip to negotiate the conditions of his investiture. The French community, whom the duke detested, could, for a time at least, breathe freely.

Either shortly before or shortly after his arrival in Ferrara in the spring of 1535, Marot contemplated martyrdom in an evangelistic epistle (*Epîtres,* XXXV) to two "sisters" (in Christ) from Savoie and in the remarkably courageous epistle to Francis I from Ferrara (*Epîtres,* XXXVI). Marot's fears, however, seemed to recede in the sheltered atmosphere of Renée's court. He once again turned to writing circumstantial and satirical pieces full of his old confidence and verve. It was from Ferrara, for example, that Marot launched the famous "Blason du beau tétin." The blason is a description designed either to praise or blame. Marot's sparkling witty poem provoked poets throughout France, including Maurice Scève, to write blasons on different parts of the body.

Ercole's return to Ferrara in January 1536 brought an end to this happy life. Renée's reformist sentiments became more pronounced and Ercole was convinced that Michelle de Saubonne was at fault. Despite pressures from Francis I to the contrary, he ordered her to leave in the spring of 1536. Marot wrote two epistles for the occasion—one, (*Epîtres,* XL) for Michelle de Saubonne, another, (*Epîtres,* XLI) for her daughter Renée de Parthenay. After her friends' departure, Renée locked herself up in her apartments and refused to appear at court, not only because of her anger, but also out of fear of being poisoned. To make matters worse, on 14 April, a month after Michelle de Saubonne's departure, Jehannet, who had come to Ferrara with Marot and Jamet, shrugged his shoulders and walked out of church at the moment of the elevation during the Good Friday Mass. Jehannet, also known as Zanetto, was turned over to the Inquisition; his attitude hurt the cause of the French reformists in Ferrara. Marot, as the most notorious of the French "Lutherans" at the court, found himself in a situation in which he had as much to fear from Ercole as he had from Francis I after *l'affaire des placards.* He was put on the inquisitor's list and fled Ferrara around 1 June 1536. He left behind only a hasty but moving epistle of excuse and sympathy to Madame de Ferrare (*Epîtres,* XLII).

   **Venice.** Marot chose Venice for several reasons. The French ambassador to that city, Georges de Selve, was in Ferrara at the time and probably encouraged the poet to go there. Furthermore,

Venice was noted for its religious tolerance. As a crossroads between the Christian and Muslim worlds, it was more interested in commercial advantages than in religious orthodoxy. It had long been a refuge to reformers, who took advantage of its printing presses—among the first and probably most extensive in Italy—to turn out translations of the Bible as well as other religious works.

Upon his arrival, Marot sent Renée another epistle (*Epîtres,* XLIII) in which he comments on the city's splendor—already in its present-day form—from the perspective of a shocked reformed Christian. The virulently evangelical tendencies of certain sections of the poem are most striking. In fact, when Marot included the epistle in a manuscript he prepared for Anne de Montmorency in 1538, he struck them out so as not to offend the devout Catholicism of the Connétable.

Marot also wrote an epigram to Renée, which may well be the first sonnet ever written in French (*O.D.,* CLXXVII). There he implies that the persecutions are about to end either because he believed that reform within the church was gaining ground, or perhaps because he was referring to the new atmosphere of tolerance apparent in France. Francis I's cruelty had been inspired partly by political fears, partly by Pope Clement VII. The new Pope Paul III, however, who had come to the throne in 1534, was much more conciliatory. "It is a cruel death to burn a man alive," he told the king. Francis had a change of heart and issued a series of edicts culminating in the May 1536 general amnesty.

Yet Marot did not seem to trust the terms of the edicts and began a letter-writing campaign from Venice. Three of the poems (*O.L.,* LXXVI, *Epîtres,* XLIV, and XLVI) are deeply personal, heartrending cries for help that echo Ovid's *Tristia* and *Ex Ponto.* The *Suite* had contained the first significant collection of elegies in name to appear in French, but these three poems achieve elegy in act. Marot also wrote a request to the dauphin, asking him to intercede with the king. The epistle is lighter, more like Marot's "élégant badinage," but nevertheless touching and in some respects very serious. Unfortunately, the dauphin suddenly died from chills when he drank cold water from a pitcher after a hard game of tennis (*paume*). Rumor had it that he had been poisoned by an agent from Charles V, who had recently invaded Provence. The dauphin's poor cupbearer, Montecuculi, paid for these suspicions with his life. Marot wrote a short epitaph for the dauphin and alluded to the incident in the fourth

coq-à-l'âne, which, with the third, was also written in Venice. Especially interesting is the third coq-à-l'âne in which this born-again
Christian, writing from a *basochien* tavern, rips into Béda, Sagon,
and the horrors of the war in Provence with unmitigated scorn and
mockery.

**Attacks from François Sagon.**   The allusions to Sagon—against
whom Marot had drawn a dagger during Isabelle de Navarre's wedding—refer to a dastardly act of revenge. Sagon saw in Marot's
epistles to Francis I and the Savoisien sisters—whom Sagon thought
to be from Paris—an opportunity either to supplant Marot as court
poet outright or at least to attract the attention of the lettered
world. Sagon replied to Marot's epistles with his "Coup d'essai,"
actually a collection of poems that Sagon presented to Francis I.
The title of the collection was drawn from Marot's preface to the
*Adolescence clémentine*. There it will be recalled, Marot had presented
his collection of youthful works as a *coup d'essai*.

Sagon's answer is a mixture of pretension and groveling false
modesty that makes one appreciate all the more the delicate balance
Marot achieves between learning, humility, and poetic dignity
throughout his career. Slander and bad poetry aside, the "Coup
d'essai" does advance real arguments that defend establishment forces
outside the court. In reply to Marot's profession of faith, Sagon says
that Marot appropriates the name of Christian, but is in fact a
Lutheran and a heretic. A devout Roman Catholic, Sagon had little
sympathy for the religious syncretisms of court circles. In defense
of the Sorbonne, Sagon answers that Marot is not sufficiently in-
structed to criticize that venerable institution which, inspired by
God and the Holy Spirit, receives the fruit of the Bible like manna
from heaven. As for Justice, Sagon says that Marot attacks her
servants because they are not taken in by his deceitful writing. He
points out that Marot has eaten meat during Lent and has harbored
forbidden books to which he pretentiously considers himself immune.

**Return home.**   Despite the efforts of such rivals, Marot was
finally allowed to return to France, but only under the normal
conditions of the royal amnesty. He had to abjure. He arrived in
Lyon from Venice at the beginning of December 1536 and addressed
an epistle (*Epîtres*, XLVII) of salutation to the city and the cardinal
of Tournon, who was to conduct the abjuration ceremony. Most
humiliating must have been the moment on 14 December when
Marot was stripped "usque and camisam" and constrained to remain

kneeling at the door of St. Jean's Cathedral while being flagellated
to the words of Psalms 51 ("Miserere mei, Deus") and 67 ("Dominus
miseratur"). The force of the blows was measured according to the
gravity of Marot's offenses.

The ceremony over, Marot turned to more pleasant preoccupa-
tions. He was warmly welcomed by the men and women of letters
who so distinguished the city in the Renaissance. Most important,
he met the distinguished, if somewhat colorful, humanist Etienne
Dolet, who was setting up a press in Lyon, which was to publish
a new edition of the poet's works. Marot bid his friends farewell
(O.L., LXXVII) at the beginning of 1537, but not without a note
of bitterness. He alludes to his beating with the French proverb,
"Beat the dog in front of the Lion."

## New Glory (1537–1542)

Marot arrived in Paris in February 1537 and attended the banquet
Etienne Dolet held to celebrate the royal amnesty that pardoned
him for the killing of the painter Compaing. It was an illustrious
company that included Rabelais and Budé. On 8 March, Marot
returned to the court which he salutes with his famous "Dieu Garde
de Marot à la Cour de France" (O.L., LXXVIII). The return was
not without its administrative difficulties, however. Epigrams
CXLIX, CL, CXCIII, and CCII of the Mayer edition refer to a
campaign for back wages like that of 1527 in which Marot had to
pressure administrators to carry out the king's orders. Once such
matters were settled, the poet reassumed his role as court poet.

**Settling scores with Sagon.**   Sagon's libel, mentioned above,
had set off a major poetic quarrel. According to Guiffrey, the true
issue was court patronage. Poets outside the court were attempting
to displace Marot, who had been in disgrace. Marot, now back in
favor, answered with the "Epître de Frippelippes" (O.S., VI). There
he pretends that it is his valet Frippelippes who answers Sagon since
a reply to such a second-rate poet is hardly worthy of the master
himself. The epistle set off a round of poetic replies on both sides
that are often little more than obscene insults. Marot, however,
wrote no more except for an epigram (Epig.,CXCV), never published, where he accuses Sagon of always copying him like a monkey.
The affair finally subsided.

The rest of the poetry that Marot wrote in 1537 dealt mainly with illnesses (Francis I, Henri d'Albret) and voyages (Francis I, Princesse Jeanne de Navarre, Marguerite, Henri d'Albret). **1538: The Montmorency manuscript.** There is very little precise information on Marot in 1538. It is generally assumed that he followed the court and that his center of operations was Lyon at least from March to July. On 10 February 1538, Anne de Montmorency had been elevated to the rank of Connétable de France—the position previously held by François de Bourbon. In March, Marot presented the powerful man with a manuscript of previously unpublished works, most of which had been composed either at Ferrara or afterwards. Montmorency placed the manuscript in his collection at Chantilly where it remains to this day. The manuscript is important. It contains versions of the verse epistles written from exile in which Marot tones down his previous evangelistic fervor so as not to offend the sensibilities of the staunchly Catholic Montmorency. It also contains pieces that Marot never published afterwards such as the biting epigram against Sagon. Finally it is in the Chantilly manuscript that Marot first uses the term *epigram,* which he applies to eighty-one poems of his own invention and eleven imitated from Martial. The Montmorency manuscript is one of the two authoritative versions of Marot's collected works. The other is the one that Dolet published in 1538.

 **The 1538 Dolet edition of the collected works.** In July 1538 Marot wrote a prose epistle to Dolet that served as the preface to the new edition. There (*Epîtres,* pp. 91–94) Marot lashes out against editors who printed false editions of his works during his exile, mainly because they mixed poorly written and seditious works with his own in an effort to increase their profits. The effect of their editions, he says, was to besmirch his reputation and make his return to France more difficult. Now, he says, the present edition is ampler and more clearly arranged.

 The order of the poems in the 1538 edition is very much like that of the old. One still finds *L'Adolescence clémentine* and *La Suite.* Both are greatly augmented, but Marot does not go so far as to include "Hell," his most controversial poem, the epistles written from exile, and the psalms he had already translated. At the end of the edition, Marot also includes his translation of the first book of Ovid's *Métamorphoses.*

The greatest innovation, however, is the addition of two books of epigrams. Marot places there all the shorter pieces he had included previously in the *Adolescence* and *La Suite,* most of the epigrams from the Chantilly manuscript, and several others written in 1537–38. These poems give glimmers of Marot's urbane and sophisticated life at the courts of Marguerite, the king, and Renée.

Subsequent Dolet editions are generally considered to have been done without Marot's consent. In fact, there seems to have been a falling out between the two shortly after the publication of the Dolet edition, because only a few months afterwards Gryphius published a nearly identical edition. In place of epigrams dedicated to Dolet one finds two bitingly satirical pieces (*Epig.,* XLIX and L). In one of these, Marot says that he has taken his enemy out of his work and hopes that the latter will do the same.

By the end of 1538, Marot was at the height of his success. In the "Eglogue to the King" (*O.L.,* LXXXIX), he optimistically promises that if he can be assured of a place to live, he will write poetry as has never before been seen. Francis I granted his request in July 1539 with the gift of a house—"la maison du cheval de bronze"—in Paris. Marot's future seemed assured.

**Poems regarding relations with Charles V.** In the meantime, Francis I and Charles V continued their rivalries and reconciliations. Francis I had conquered Savoie and the Piedmont, reducing the duke of Savoie to the fortress of Nice. In return, Charles V had invaded Provence only to be repulsed by Montmorency's scorched-earth defense, the first in history. A series of negotiations followed, including Pope Paul II, Montmorency, and Charles V's sister, Maria of Hungary. Yet the only result was a truce, not a treaty. Thus when the emperor asked for permission to cross through France with an army to go to punish the rebellious citizens of Gand in Flanders, France accepted only after great hesitation. In January 1540, Marot published the major poems he had written for these matters in *Les Cantiques de la Paix,* which recall the French desires for peace. Marot also, at the request of Francis I, presented the emperor with a manuscript of thirty psalms translated into French.

**From glory to exile.** The year 1541 began well enough with "Les Etrennes aux Dames de la Cour," forty-one brilliant diamonds of wit offered to various ladies of the court to wish them well for the New Year. In June 1541, Jeanne d'Albret was to marry the duke of Clèves. A tournament, the *Tournoi des chevaliers errants,* was held near Châtellerault during the festivities. Marot wrote six epigrams, (*Epig.*, CCXII–CCXVII) for this which served as inscriptions for the marble bases (*perrons*), on which the knights stood. However, Marot never once mentions the marriage, which took place against the princess's will and was never to be consummated. The pieces are interesting from a historical point of view because they were the precursor of Ronsard's "Mascarades, combats, et cartels."

Other activities from this period include Marot's translations of Musaeus's *Leander and Hero,* the second book of *Metamorphoses,* and Erasmus's colloquies. Marot may also have written Epistle LIII— an exhortation to renounce love—as a contribution to the *querelle des amies.* This quarrel pitted sixteenth-century feminists against antifeminists around the question of whether women could love without reference to material considerations.

Precise knowledge of Marot's whereabouts is not available for 1541–42. By the end of 1542, however, the poet's fortune had so declined that he was forced once again to flee into exile. One legend—now discredited—had it that he insulted Francis I's mistress, the duchesse d'Etampes. Another story comes from Calvin, who, in a letter to Viret, says that Marot was on his way home from court when he was warned to flee because the Parlement had issued a warrant for his arrest. It would seem that the publication or reedition of controversial poems in 1541–42 aroused the ire of the forces of persecution, all the stronger because Francis I had again changed sides against the reformers. (Once again the syncretists at court found themselves in the opposition.) Little did it seem to matter that some of these poems (such as "L'Enfer") were published without Marot's consent or that some ("Le Sermon du bon et du mauvais pasteur") were falsely attributed to him. Between December 1542 and March 1543 the faculty of theology condemned Marot's translation of the thirty psalms and the "Sermon." Where to flee?

## Exile Again

Calvin, whom Marot had met in Ferrara, had just led Geneva's revolt against the duke of Savoie and was setting up an independent citadel of a new reformed church. By the end of 1542 he was compiling poems, prayers, and hymns to be used in the services and assemblies of the faithful. Calvin welcomed Marot to Geneva, hoping that he would finish translating all the psalms into French.

The poet accepted the invitation probably more out of material considerations than from flaming conviction in the reformed faith. He desperately needed financial support and safe refuge.

Marot arrived in Geneva in November or early December 1542. The Pastor Malingre welcomed him in a long verse epistle in which he calls the poet to the austere ways of the new faith. The worldly, witty Marot was hardly pleased by such a welcome as is indicated by his cold, polite eight-lined reply (*Epig.*, CCXXVI).

**The psalms.**   Once in Geneva Marot worked closely with Calvin, revising the thirty psalms he had already translated. Furthermore, Calvin wrote the preface for a new edition dated June 1543 in which he sets forth the principles for a liturgy in French. Yet Marot was not completely won over to Calvin's version of religious reform as indicated by the edition he proposed to Geneva's council in June 1543—an edition that included, of all things, the Hail Mary! Nor did he ever forget France. In March 1543, he wrote an epigram to Francis I, recalling that it was the king who had encouraged him to begin the translation. Indeed, Marot's psalm translations had originally been a court, not a Calvinist, project probably going back to Luigi Alamanni's publication of seven translated psalms in his 1532 *Opere toscane*. In August, Marot published a French edition which Dolet prefaced with a dedication to the ladies of the court, enjoining them to sing the psalms. The psalms were still popular at the court of France where Francis I himself, who had fallen ill, was given to singing them.

Although Marot's heart remained in France, his collaboration with Calvin was not hypocritical, but a manifestation of the pre-1534 movement that we associate with court evangelism. Until the "confessional divorce" came around 1560, tolerant Catholics and reformers could and did collaborate on psalm translations based on Marot's original poems and methods, often in the hope of maintaining or reviving pre-1534 ideals of a nonschismatic evangelical reform. For example, the *Colloque de Poissy* granted a royal privilege to the Calvinist Théodore de Bèze's edition of 150 psalm translations that included Marot's original forty-nine. Once confessional divorce did come, however, Marot's translations were too widely used by the Calvinists to be acceptable to Catholics. Thus, it is the fortunes of the work that make Marot a Calvinist rather than the work itself. Here, as in his other religious works, Marot was a victim of his writings.

Marot was unhappy in Geneva. The city was stingy. When it became clear that financial remuneration was not forthcoming, Marot stopped all work for the reform except for an epigram against Rome which he never published. By the end of 1543 he had left. Théodore de Bèze said that Marot's past life at the French court made him ill-suited for the ways of Geneva.

**Adrift.**   Now Marot had no place to go. Like Meliboeus in Virgil's first eclogue, he was condemned to wander and beg. An epigram (*Epig.*, CCXXVIII) and an epistle (*Epîtres*, LVI) bear traces of short stays at the châteaux of Longefan and Bellegarde. His last permanent residence was Chambéry, where manuscripts of three apocryphal religious poems were said to be found.

The other poems written in this period are attempts to gain protection at court. In these, Marot is either archaic or ultramodern, depending on his audience. A long complaint for Guillaume Preud-homme (*O.L.*, IX) is a thinly veiled attempt to win the good graces of the treasurer's son that revives Rhétoriqueur conventions Marot had long abandoned. An eclogue (*O.L.*, XC) written to celebrate the birth of the dauphin to Catherine de Médicis is an early example of the lofty high style that Ronsard and the Pléiade will write under Henry II. Marot also wrote epigrams to Francis I denouncing Geneva (*Epig.*, CCXXIX) and asking for money to translate the third book of Ovid's *Metamorphoses* (*Epig.*, CCXXXIV). Finally, he wrote an epigram (*Epig.*, CCXXXI) and an epistle (*Epîtres*, LVII) to François d'Enghien who was at Ceresole in Piedmont to confront imperial forces. Both the eclogue and the epistle are deeply moving because we hear behind the pleas for support the cry of a frustrated poet who is at the height of his powers but is hindered by material difficulties. "Neither Orpheus, Apollo, Clio, Pan, nor Syrinx will be able to outdo me if I can only live long enough," he says in the eclogue. "I shall be France's new Homer," he promises in the epistle.

Support was never to come, however. Marot was to be neither Orpheus nor Homer. After his visit to Ceresole, he went to Turin where he died in September 1544. His faithful friend Lyon Jamet had him buried at the Ospidale San Giovanni Battista, but even here he was not to find peace. The Inquisition removed all traces of his tomb, and we do not know where Marot finally found a place to rest.

# Chapter Two
# Hierarchies

## Levels of Style: High, Middle, Low

The classical hierarchy of styles—high, middle, and low—is far from well-defined and unchanging. Cicero and Quintilian originally intended it for oratory, not poetry, and by the thirteenth century, the famous wheel of Virgil bases the distinction on subject matter and social class rather than qualities of diction.[1] Here the shepherd and things pastoral on the model of Virgil's eclogues constitute the low style, things agricultural as in Virgil's *Georgics* belong to the middle style, and things military such as are treated in the *Aeneid* belong to the high style. By the Renaissance, the low style in literature (*genus subtile, tenue,* or *extenuatum*) came to be associated with factual narration, argumentation, proverbs, and common wisdom. Poetic genres associated with the low style are the epistle, epigram, satire, eclogue, and elegy.[2] Middle style poetry delights and conciliates. It is flowing yet flowery. Although there are no genres traditionally associated with it, J. Houston has shown that Petrarch's lyrics were considered a model of the middle style, as is the ornamentation associated with mannerist and baroque poetry. The high style is intended to move its audience through forceful means and bold ornament. Its major genres are the ode, the epic, and tragedy. Clearer definitions of these categories will be given later in the course of our study.

Marot spent most of his artistic life elaborating the low style. He is best remembered for his epistles and epigrams. He is the first poet to write eclogues and a collection of elegies in French. His coqs-à-l'âne are good examples of low style satire. Some of his poetry, as we shall see, tends toward high or middle, but more often than not, nonchalantly breaks decorum with low style intrusions.

## Opuscules and Translations

In this respect, the 1538 edition which we are following in this study is very interesting because it begins with five long works arranged in hierarchical order: four translations, and the "Temple de Cupidon," ("Temple of Cupid"). Beginning with Constantin in 1544, modern editors usually put the "Temple of Cupid" in a section called "opuscules"—long poems with no specific generic designation. They class the other four poems with Marot's translations. However, modern editors have overlooked the hierarchical order from lowest to highest as determined by content: pastoral, love, war, religion. Thus it is important to study these poems together in the 1538 sequence. In this order, they outline the major areas of subject matter in Marot's collection, and they show that from the very beginning Marot worked with distinctions of hierarchy and genre.

The first poem in the series is Marot's translation of Virgil's first eclogue (*T.*, I). Critics and scholars usually point out the poor quality of the translation and recall Marot's weak or even nonexistent grasp of Latin. The decasyllabic line is considered insufficient to render the flow of Virgil's hexameter, and Marot is condemned for almost doubling the length of the original. Past scholars, however, have probably been too harsh on Marot and may well be reacting more to the pre-Ronsardian poetic diction of the early sixteenth century than to Marot's art as a translator. H. Guy, for example, criticizes Marot for translating *villa* by *cité*.[3] Yet Marot is rendering the medieval Latin meaning of the word. The poem should be judged in terms of its success as a piece of pastoral poetry rather than as an accurate translation. For Marot still practices medieval forms of imitation and translation which adapt to one's own culture rather than simply transpose. The pastoral is traditionally of the low or plain style. Marot's translation flows well in French and is free of Rhétoriqueur ornament. Its relative simplicity is appropriate to a French version of the genre.

Scholars have overlooked the fact that Marot's choice of the eclogue to open the *Adolescence* is a significant poetic act. Virgil's poem is generally considered to have a covert meaning as a celebration of the young Octavian's (Augustus) reinstatement of the farm that Virgil had lost in the civil war. The poem presents a contrast between Tityrus, who sings and works on his ancestral lands because of a god (Augustus) in Rome, and Meliboeus, who, not knowing that god, is forced to leave his lands and wander the earth. To call a ruler a god is more than just decorative metaphor. It stems from a very ancient theory, euhemerism, which tried to give a rational explanation for the Greek and Roman gods. It held that "traditional deities are merely earthly rulers whom gratitude or adulation of their subjects has caused to place in heaven," and it led to the practice of deifying Roman emperors at their death.[4]

The eclogue's place at the beginning of Marot's edition allows it to function as a subtle nod to Francis I, Marot's patron. Just as Augustus had brought about a renewal of Greek learning in Latin guise, so now the French monarchy was trying to renew Roman glory in French. The theory behind this is usually referred to as *renovatio imperii* (renewal of empire).[5] Thus, it was enough for Marot to recall Virgil's dependence on Augustus to imply, without direct comment, his own dependence as the new Virgil on the god in Paris, the new Augustus, Francis I. He also implies his awareness that without Francis I, he could well—as indeed he did—suffer the fate of Meliboeus. Marot will return to the pastoral mode later in life when dealing with questions of patronage. The "Eclogue sur la mort de Louise de Savoie" laments the loss of a patroness and protectress. The "Eglogue au roi" is a request for lodging. The "Eglogue sur la naissance du dauphin" implies a desperate wish to return from exile. Furthermore, when Marot speaks of himself as a poet, he often adopts a pastoral guise, notably in the poem "L'Enfer" ("Hell"). Thus, although the first poem in the *Adolescence* is a translation, it prefigures Marot's use of pastoral conventions throughout his poetic career to express his dependence on the monarchy.

The "Temple of Cupid" (*O.L.,* I) is an allegorical poem about love. It is a notch in the generic hierarchy above pastoral but below war poetry. In the 1538 edition, Marot addresses it to Nicolas de Neufville, the man who suggested he write it and present it to the king. In earlier editions, however, Marot prefaces the poem with a dedication to Francis I in which he evokes the poem's didactic usefulness. Just as the prince should learn arms, he also should learn true—not only physical—love so as to have a more generous heart than Alexander and gain the love of all people.

The poem is written with the full panoply of allegorical devices inherited from the *Romance of the Rose* and the Rhétoriqueurs. Its more ornamented style is appropriate to its higher place in the generic hierarchy. Scholars have generally acknowledged Jean Lemaire's "Temple of Venus" from *La Concorde des deux langages* as Marot's major source. Other sources are Alain Chartier's "Hôpital d'Amour," Molinet's "Temple de Mars," Coquillart's "Droits nouveaux," and Ovid's *Metamorphoses* and *Art of Love*. C.A. Mayer is only partially correct in refuting earlier scholars with the assertion that Marot borrows relatively little from Lemaire's "Temple of Venus."[6] It is true that there are few direct imitations of lines and phrases, but the earlier scholarly perception is correct to the extent that Lemaire's poem is the only one of Marot's immediate predecessors that points out the treacherous deceit of love's charm and beauty. The poet of *La Concorde* rejects the temple of Venus for the temple of Minerva, goddess of wisdom.[7] Marot, as we shall see, imitates general structures more than individual lines and phrases.

The "Temple of Cupid" Christianizes Lemaire's poem. Instead of wisdom, the narrator seeks the *Ferme Amour* (Steadfast Love) of Christian charity. At the beginning of the poem, Cupid takes off his blindfold to survey the extent of his kingdom. He sees that all are under his sway except the poet who goes so far as to shun love even in his verse. As a revenge, Cupid shoots the poet with an arrow of unrequited love, which causes such great suffering that the poet decides to take a long journey in order to forget his passion and to seek the higher Steadfast Love. After much vain travel, the poet decides to seek Steadfast Love in the temple of Cupid. The journey to the temple and the description of the temple itself is an allegory in the classical sense of the term. It is an extended metaphor that strikes an analogy primarily between the religion of love and the religion of Christ, but also between the temple and a garden. Marot encounters Love's pilgrims who erect roadside shrines along the way. The temple itself is a beautiful garden peopled with personified abstractions, such as Danger and Fair Welcome. It is a version of the *hortus conclusus* (enclosed garden) that opens the *Romance of the Rose*. It is also peopled with the gods of Greek and Roman mythology. The description is quite detailed. Above the door are Cupid's arms and image. Fair Welcome guards the first door made out of red flowers, but Danger guards a door made of thorns behind.

Once inside the temple, the poet carefully surveys the interior, beginning with the high altar and moving forward toward the entrance. Then he goes into more detail and describes various rituals. The poet at first delights in all of this and visits everywhere until he realizes that there is no Peace on the altar—Venus and Cupid make war on humanity. Wondering whether he is in Heaven or Hell, he begins to wander about the nave where lovers are hunting different animals. There he sees two sorts of love that he rejects:

physical love (*amour vénérienne*) and fickle love (*fol' amour*). He despairs, thinking that Steadfast Love—which he defines as Christian charity—must not exist in the temple. On looking through the door of the choir, however, he falls back because there he sees Steadfast Love presiding over Francis I and his new wife Claude. He goes in to serve her and concludes with a good Rhétoriqueur pun that Steadfast Love is "au coeur éprouvée" (experienced in the heart/choir, {1. 537]).

Past scholars have generally been severe on the poem. For them, the mixture of Olympus with allegorical personifications, the rhetorical wordplay, the mechanical nature of the allegorical apparatus make this poem little more than the exercise of a beginning poet. They find particularly incongruous the extended comparison between the temple of Cupid and the temple of Christ. But their explanations are disappointing. P. Villey assures us that Marot has no irreverent intention but is simply following tradition.[8] H. Guy considers the procedure a stylistic game, P. Jourda and C.A. Mayer, bad taste.[9] P. Leblanc calls it "perfectly innocent" and R. Griffin, an example of the Renaissance fluidity between *eros* and *ecclesia* (erotic love and church).[10] P.M. Smith comments that it is difficult not to consider certain correspondences as comic.[11] Such explanations, however, gloss over the didactic nature of the poem. Indeed, read from a certain perspective, the poet is neither incongruous, irreverent, nor guilty because of his extended comparison between eros and ecclesia; however, the personages he describes participating in this drama certainly are, for they have idolatrously replaced Christ with Cupid. Like all idolatry, theirs is one of superficially dazzling, paradisiac beauty and promises fulfillment. But the poet—like his predecessor Jean Lemaire—soon learns that such impressions are only illusions. The rose has thorns. What seems at first to be heaven turns out to be hell. The minute detail of the description conveys how far-reaching the idolatry of love can actually be, for it sets up a full-fledged antichurch. From this perspective, many of the comic incongruities are touches of condemning irony—for example, the naked ladies bathing in baptismal fonts attended to by their lovers (ll. 303–12). We smile at such usurpation of Christian practice because it is so unashamed. The poem is full of such didactic wit.

Only in the heart of the temple (ll. 496–538), the choir, does Marot find the nonidolatrous Steadfast Love based on Christian charity. It is neither fickle nor just physical because it is marital love as exemplified between the king and queen of France. To consider such a reference as mere flattery is an oversimplification. As a didactic work, the poem counsels the king and queen to find Steadfast Love in their marriage as well as it flatters them for having already found it. Furthermore, by defining this marital love as belonging to Christian charity and giving it the central place in the temple, Marot indicates the perspective from which the other kinds of love can find their proper expression. Thus the "Temple of Cupid" is counsel as well as praise and confirmation.

The "Jugement de Minos" ("Judgment of Minos") (*T.*, II), the next poem in the collection, is a translation of Lucian's twelfth dialogue of the dead. Marot wrote this translation before the "Temple of Cupid," but places it afterwards in the *Adolescence* according to good hierarchical logic. It rises up a notch above love poetry. Actually, Marot knew no Greek but follows Jean Miélot's fifteenth-century prose version of the dialogue, which is itself probably based on a Latin translation of the Italian humanist, Aurispa. [12]

In the poem, Alexander, Hannibal, and Scipio ask Minos to judge who among them is the greatest. Minos decides in favor of Scipio because the Roman observed peaceful as well as warlike virtues. The piece closes with a warning to the other two to realize the outrageous nature of their desire for bloodshed and reminds them that courage without Reason is not a virtue.

Like the eclogue, this poem should not be judged solely as a translation. Rather, it is a piece of writing that reproduces bits of epic narration—the highest of the classical genres. The oratorical tone that the three heroes establish before the judge is also more exalted than either the descriptive narration of the "Temple of Cupid" or the shepherd's speeches in the pastoral.

Furthermore, the philosophy of war that the poem outlines fits meaningfully into the sequence that opens the *Adolescence*. It is a discussion of virtue that follows the traditional categorization—deeds of war and deeds of peace. [13] Deeds of war are signs of courage and good fortune. The virtue of courage, however, is in itself not enough. A truly great man—the traditional view is sexist—also practices peaceful virtues. He exercises courage with wisdom.

The next two poems in the section are "Les Tristes Vers de Philippe Béroalde sur le jour du vendredi saint" ("Philip Beroaldus's Sad Verses on the Day of Good Friday,") (*T.*, IV) and "Oraison contemplative devant le crucifix" ("Contemplative Prayer in front of the Crucifix") (*T.*, III).[14] (The titles are self-explanatory.) Critics have puzzled over why Marot chose to translate these two poems. They do, however, fill out the classical hierarchy, rising from the realm of heroism to Christian religion. Both share in the excessive and exaggerated imagery of the times that prefigures the baroque, although later in the century they would be considered middle-style poems. Here their boldness, as opposed to the subtle ironies of the "Temple of Cupid," perhaps marks a high-style intent.

The most striking departure from the original is Marot's shortened version of the call to joy that ends Beroaldus's poem. Perhaps the arrangement of the poems in the *Adolescence* called Marot to do so in order to smooth the transition to Loches's in the *Adolescence*. Taken together, the two poems outline the major events on the Christian road to salvation: acceptance of death (first poem), prayer for grace, confession of sin, repentance, and hope. Beroaldus's original call to joy at the end of the first poem would have obscured the sequence.

In doctrinal terms, the two poems fall well into the realm of Catholic orthodoxy. In the first, Marot's rather exaggerated "baroque" fascination with exterior manifestations of mourning and repentance participates in waning medieval cultic practices. In the second, the poet's observation that God created women, riches, food, wine, and long nights is considered to undermine his confession in which he shows that monogamy (not celibacy, as some have suggested), fasting, humility, and work are also divinely ordained. However, the *pro* and *contra* form of this confession is an example of scholastic dialectic in which both sides of a question are presented.[15] G. Guiffrey sees in the negative side of the dialectic an evangelistic condemnation of celibacy and fasting.[16] The dialectic, however, opposes not celibacy to sexuality but—like the "Temple of Cupid"—unrestrained sexuality to one tamed in the context of monogamy. In fact, the second poem is even more orthodox than the original, for unlike Loches, Marot calls for prayer to the saints and considers marriage a sacrament. The poems should be read as descriptions of the Christian life experience, which often embraces contradictory attitudes, rather than as statements of unconflicted dogma.

Actually, all five poems that open the *Adolescence* share in the dialectical method of the last in that they compare different ways of life. Virgil's first eclogue compares the life of loyal Tityrus to wandering Meliboeus's who does not know the god in Rome. The

"Temple of Cupid" compares physical love, fickle love, and marital love. The "Judgment of Minos" compares the virtuous Scipio with the war captains, Alexander and Hannibal. Beroaldus's verses on Good Friday, with the anti-Semitism typical of the era, compare those who mourn Christ's death with unrepentant Jews who continue to be guilty of it. And the "Contemplative Prayer" juxtaposes the intellectual positions for and against monogamy, fasting, and vigils. Marot does come out strongly for one side: loyalty to the god in Rome, marital love, warlike courage accompanied by other virtues, acceptance of death, and a call for confession and repentance. The result of the five poems is an enunciation of a basic philosophy concerning the five major areas of Renaissance experience: poetry, patronage, love, heroism, and religion.

It is difficult to assess the function of these poems in Marot's collection. Because of their clear position at the beginning of the *Adolescence,* the opening poems are a counterweight to Marot's lighter poetry. On one level, they imply that the lighter writings are but expressions of transitory experiences in a very human life that includes delightful sin and reversal of fortune on the road to faith in God and virtue. The Marot who writes a scabrous rondeau reminds one of the boy who joyously embarked on the road to Cupid's temple; the Marot who breaks Lent recalls the protests against fasting before the crucifix; and the poet who writes to the king from Ferrara shares the fate of Meliboeus as well as Tityrus. Nevertheless, on another level, the five opening poems share in Marot's fascination with the opposition, as it were, despite their clearly stated orthodoxy and political conservatism. We shall frequently return to this fascination throughout the following study.

# Chapter Three
# Epistles of the *Adolescence*

Marot most owes his lasting reputation to his verse epistles, which span his entire career. Both the *Adolescence* and the *Suite* contain collections of epistles. Another group written during the poet's 1534–36 exile in Italy appears in the Chantilly manuscript. In addition, there are epistles Marot never included in any collection: satirical epistles—three of the four coqs-à-l'âne and the famous epistle written against Marot's archenemy François Sagon—as well as a handful of others. Marot's last epistle, which celebrates François de Bourbon's victory at Ceresole in 1544, was written a few months before the poet's death. Marot practices a wide variety of styles in the epistles, but the most famous is a low style to which Boileau's term *élégant badinage* does much injustice. It is witty and suggests a natural conversational idiom. The epistles to Lyon Jamet and Bouchard are the two poems in the *Adolescence* representative of this style, which we shall call "plain."

Marot's epistles rest on two traditions: that of medieval rhetorical epistolary theory (*ars dictaminis*) and that constituted by the practice of Marot's immediate predecessors, the Rhétoriqueurs. Past scholarship on the relation between Marot and epistolary theory has been limited to a consideration of Sebillet's *Art poétique* and rhetorical treatises in E. Langlois's collection.[1] In both cases, however, only passing reference is made to the epistle in conjunction with love poetry. Thus, scholars have done little more than to point out that Marot's elegies, which are love poems, are types of epistles. Sebillet's discussion is particularly difficult to follow. He considers elegies to be love epistles and then tries to distinguish them from epistles about love that are not elegies. Love epistles that are not elegies for Sebillet belong to the tradition of Ovid's *Heroides,* whereas elegies belong to the tradition of Ovid's *Amores.* Then he says, "l'Elégie traite l'Amour . . . mais simplement et nuement: où l'épître garde sa forme de superscriptions et souscriptions, et de style plus populaire" (The Elegy deals with Love . . . but simply and directly: whereas the epistle keeps its form of superscriptions and subscriptions, and its form of popular style).[2] We shall see later in this chapter that Sebillet's distinctions are useful but need clarification. A better source of epistolary theory is Pierre Fabri's *Grand et vrai art de pleine rhétorique,* which went through six editions between 1521 and 1544. It contains quite an extensive section on the art of letter writing that allows many insights into Marot's method.[3] Fabri defines the epistle quite simply as the act of speaking to someone who is absent and telling that person what one wants. The type of epistle one writes is intimately bound up with whether the addressee is of a higher, equal, or lesser station in life than the sender. Furthermore, there are three estates: the great, such as pope, emperor, or king; the middle, such as priests and bourgeois; and finally the low, such as servants, laborers, and so on. This hierarchy—reminiscent of the famous medieval wheel of Virgil, which also links the level of style to social class—establishes the epistle as a genre that can accommodate a wide range of styles.

Furthermore, according to Fabri, epistles are divided into three parts: cause, intention, and conclusion. The cause contains the reasons for writing; the intention expresses the sender's will; and the conclusion draws the consequences. Fabri correlates this tripartite division with the six parts of the Ciceronian oration: exordium, narration, division, confirmation, confutation, and conclusion. The cause includes confirmation and confutation, and the conclusion is a common term for both schema.

After introducing this battery of terminology, Fabri then says that only narration and petition—a new term—are absolutely necessary, for in the narration one states the facts and in the petition one declares one's will. Petition, it should be noted, is a shorthand term interchangeable with confirmation and confutation as Brunetto Latini's *Livre du Trésor* explicitly states.[4] In any case, Marot's developed epistles usually follow only a simplified model: exordium, narration, petition, and conclusion. Sometimes they are even further limited to being either extended salutations, narrations, or petitions.

The epistles from the *Adolescence* follow a hierarchical arrangement except that those featuring women come beforehand. Marot as Marguerite's secretary was more closely associated with the female side of the royal family at the time. The epistle from Maguelonne to Pierre de Provence (*O.L.,* II) is first because it is a letter that a princess writes to a prince. Then come three letters that Marot, a commoner, addresses to Princess Marguerite. These are arranged in chronological order. The first, "L'Epître du dépourvu" ("The Epistle of the Destitute One") is a request to enter Marguerite's service. The second and third are reports before and after battle that Marot wrote to Marguerite while accompanying her husband Charles d'Alençon during the 1521 Hainaut campaign. In the last two epistles to women, Marot writes first to a "friend" and then to an "ally." Both are presumably his equals.

The four epistles addressed to men also are arranged in hierarchical order: king, noblemen, a doctor of theology, and a court secretary. In the "Little Epistle to the King" (*Epîtres*, I), Marot wittily describes his poetic vocation and asks the king's support. Then he relates an exchange between two noblemen: Captain Bourgeon (*Epîtres*, V) and Captain Raisin (*Epîtres*, VI).

The last two epistles concern Marot's imprisonment. In the epistle to Docteur Bouchard (*Epîtres*, IX), Marot defends his orthodoxy and asks for his freedom. In the epistle to his friend Lyon Jamet (*Epîtres*, X), he tells the famous story of the lion and the rat, promising that just as the rat saved the lion, so he, Marot, will one day help Lyon if the latter saves him now.

It is traditional to treat these poems in a reconstructed chronological order, implying that Marot evolved from a stiff Rhétoriqueur style to a more natural conversational manner. The 1538 arrangement, however, is not chronological and conveys a very different impression. It establishes Marot's versatility in styles ranging from formal and serious to low and comic. Most interesting is Marot's play with styles. The poems refer to conventions according to which a formal style is appropriate to persons in the upper reaches of the hierarchy and expressed with Rhétoriqueur ornament such as personified abstractions, repetitions, and prosodic feats of skill. In the first few poems, person, style, and situation belong to a single level of formality, but afterwards Marot subtly jostles conventions from different stylistic levels together for comic effect.

## Epistles Featuring Women

These seven epistles come first, doubtless because they begin with the most formal poems of the group, even though the last two are in a more popular style. Maguelonne's epistle (*O.L.*, II) is a 224-line miniature romance whose dimensions and level of formality so recall the opuscules that V.L. Saulnier mistakenly classified it as such in his edition of the *Adolescence*. It is also the first example of Marot's creative kind of imitation, which, instead of slavishly repeating lines from a classical author, uses that author as the beginning point of a new creation. Maguelonne's epistle, which features a heroine writing to her lover, belongs to the tradition of Ovid's *Heroides* through the intermediary of Octavien de Saint-Gelais's translation called "Les XXI Epîtres d'Ovide." However, much like Gothic artists who dressed biblical characters in medieval costume, Marot "modernizes" Ovid to suit sixteenth-century tastes. The heroine of the poem comes from the medieval romance *Pierre de Provence et la belle Maguelonne*. The Ovidian convention of a woman writing to her lover overlaps with the Rhétoriqueur phenomenon that H. Guy calls an artificial epistle—one written by a dead or imaginary person.

Rhétoriqueur conventions that are signs of the poem's formality include the epistolary subscription, the poem's great length, the use of dream, set speeches, and the enumeration—without development—of mythological lovers such as Jason and Medea, Dido and Aeneas. (Later writers will develop such mythological references more thoroughly and work them more closely into the fabric of their poetry. Marot, like the Rhétoriqueurs, simply alludes to them.) In general, Maguelonne's discourse is that of a princess living a tragedy. An idea of her formality may be seen in the following lines:

> . . . Ô Fortune indécente,
> Ce n'est pas or, ni de l'heure présente
> Que tu te prends à ceux de haute touche
> Et aux loyaux. Quel' [*sic*] rancune te touche?
> Es-tu d'envie entachée & pollue
> Dont notre amour n'a été dissolue?
>
> Ô cher ami, ô coeur doux & bénin,
> Que n'ai-je pris d'Atropos le vénin
> Avecques [*sic*] toi?
> [ll. 125–33]

( . . . O indecent Fortune / It is not now, nor in the present hour / That you attack those of high station / and great loyalty. What grudge do you bear / Are you spotted and polluted with envy? / That our love was not dissolved? / O dear friend, O heart gentle and harmless, / Why did I not take the venom of Atropos / With you?)

Here the apostrophes, the periphrasis "venom of Atropos" for "death," the doubling "Now, nor in the present hour," and the zeugma that yokes the concrete "spotted" with the abstract "envy" all mark the elevated style of the poem.

The poem corresponds to Sebillet's definition insofar as it recalls Ovid's *Heroides* and has a subscription at the beginning of the poem. (It is only one of three of Marot's epistles that has a subscription.) Its formal style, however, is the very opposite of popular in every respect. We shall see below examples of love epistles in the popular style.

Anachronistic standards of realism, *bienséance,* verisimilitude, and the alternation between masculine and feminine rhymes have led scholars and critics to overlook some of the most interesting riches of this epistle. It is a touching poem based on a legend according to which Maguelonne, daughter of the king of Naples, runs away with Pierre de Provence. In the forest she falls asleep in the lap of her lover, who finds her so irresistible that he cannot refrain from caressing—but chastely—her breasts. He comes upon a pouch hidden in her bosom, opens it, and finds three rings he had given her. A bird suddenly appears and flies off with one of the rings. Pierre follows the bird to the sea and continues pursuit in a boat which is apprehended by pirates who sell him into slavery. Finally, after many years, he finds his way back to his native land. Meanwhile, Maguelonne, who never abandoned hope of finding her lover, had also gone to Pierre's Provence where she founded a hospice for lost travelers. At the end of the story, the two lovers are reunited.

In Marot's epistle, the heroine, writing from her convent, first invokes a messenger of Venus—a pigeon—to seek out her beloved and deliver the letter. Then she touchingly traces events leading up to her present situation and petitions her lover for help. Critics usually censure Marot for having Maguelonne write to a man whose whereabouts are unknown to her. However, the initial invocation clearly establishes that just as a person stranded on a desert island desperately casts messages in bottles out to sea, Maguelonne, after many years of waiting, prayerfully and pitifully entrusts her epistle to a pigeon sacred to Venus, the goddess most likely to help her.

It has also been considered shocking and unrealistic that Maguelonne narrates how Pierre fondled her breasts and spoke of her beauty while she was asleep. Here, however, is a classic example of intertextuality. Marot assumes that we all know the legend. He does not even mention the rings. Thus, only readers aware of this absence realize that Maguelonne's description is not the result of an impossible observation or the slipup of an inexperienced poet. Rather, it is a lovesick fantasy which the heroine could have built around the fact that the rings formerly hidden in her bosom are now gone. It should never be forgotten that in a Rhétoriqueur world of dream and allegory a poet can slip between memory and fantasy as silently as any modern novelist or screen director. Furthermore, the scene is not shocking because Maguelonne insists on Pierre's virtue. To recall the hierarchy of loves in the "Temple of Cupid," Pierre's caresses belong in the context of his ultimate allegiance to a purer love. This example of virtue, by the way, is another sign of the poem's elevation.

A short rondeau (*O.L.*, pp. 123–24n) follows that also achieves Rhétoriqueur elevation by its stylistic virtuosity and moral content. The beginning letters of the lines spell out *Clément Marot,* and the poem tells the end of the story by establishing Maguelonne's superiority to Dido. Unlike Dido, Maguelonne did not give in to Fortune. Thus, God sent her loved one back to her. This moralization of the Dido episode in the *Aeneid* is also a stock medieval device.

The epistle of the Destitute One (*Epîtres,* II), which Marot addresses to Marguerite, is virtually a summary of the entire Rhétoriqueur tradition.[5] Here one indication of the poem's formality is the capitalization. Allegorical personages such as Hope and Fear come to the poet in a dream (another Rhétoriqueur formal device) where he looks to Marguerite to take him out of the sea of misfortune to the Island of Honor. The structure of the poem—a linear narrative interspersed with a rondeau and a ballade—is also a device of the Rhétoriqueur high style as are the frequent prosodic acrobatics. For example, in describing his fear, Marot resorts to nine lines of vers senées where the words in each line begin with the same letter, such as "Melencolic, morne, mary, musant."

The next epistle (*Epîtres,* III), which Marot wrote from Hainaut, could have been written in the high style because it addresses a royal princess and deals with war, the traditional subject of epic poetry. Marot, however, strikes the pose of a humble, conscientious beginner reporting on matters that are too great for him. He even characterizes his letter as poorly written (l. 1), his style as "rough" (l. 138), and his epistle as a project too ambitious for his ability (l. 144). The poem, however, is to be distinguished from Marot's conversational plain style because it has a formality appropriate to its royal addressee. It is, for example, one of Marot's three epistles that have subscriptions.

As if deceived by Marot's humble pose, scholars have unjustly denigrated this poem. They have not appreciated how Marot subtly combines elevated subject matter with a humble style. The content of the poem comes from the elevated reaches of the epic tradition that looks for virtue behind appearances. Marot describes the camp at Attigny and emphasizes Alençon's abilities as a wise commander who imposes order and gives direction to his courageous, energetic troops. J. Vianey is the only critic to have anything good to say of Marot's descriptive art when he praises Marot's lively account of training maneuvers (ll. 81–98) for its judicious use of picturesque epithets, significant gestures, and witty images.[6] Others, however, have found Marot weak. They do not appreciate the fact that apart from the description of the training maneuvers, Marot concentrates on warlike virtues rather than on visual impressions for their own sake. As he lists the various commanders' camps, he tells us that the soldiers are beautiful (l. 39), noble and diligent (ll. 47–54), warlike (ll. 55–60), physically fit (ll. 61–68), and loyal to the king (ll. 69–80). Only then does he present the visual tableau of the training maneuvers to wrap up the description.

Scholars and critics also consider this epistle little more than commissioned flattery that tries to gloss over the army's unruliness and Charles d'Alençon's incompetence. Be it flattery or not, the poem is convincing because its praises are firmly anchored in the traditional ethics of Western epic. As E.R. Curtius has shown, beginning with Homer there tends to be a dichotomy between the warrior's unbridled courage (e.g., the wrath of Achilles) and controlled, ordered wisdom (Nestor).[7] Thus Marot on the one hand glowingly describes the camp's raucous soldiers who are so eager to do battle that they kill one another in their leisure time and, on the other hand, praises Alençon for controlling this energy—the duke threatened to cut off the hands of anyone who fought with weapons! The duke is also shown to hold all together by love and to be a mentor to all who gather in his bedroom to discuss strategy. Thus whether or not Alençon was competent in military matters per se is beside the point. Marot presents him as a ruler of men who channels their energies to the good. Here, as in the "Temple of Cupid," there is a hierarchy of values rather than a conflict. The savage, warlike energies of a soldier are good when dominated by wisdom and love. The poem is an elevated meditation on the virtues of courage, bodily excellence, and wisdom.

There is an even greater discrepancy between style and subject matter in the prose epistle (*Epîtres,* Appendix I) that follows in the 1538 edition. Here Marot deals with actual battles, but abandons verse altogether. The epistle has been unjustly relegated to appendixes or placed elsewhere in modern editions. The fact that it has no exordium, but plunges right into the narration (ll. 1–27) shows that it continues the discourse begun in the preceding epistle. In the first part of the narration, Marot announces the French victory over the imperial troops at Escaut, which he attributes to Francis I's inspiration. The king is said to have so uplifted the hearts of his men that they would not only have fought but have struck out at the rest of the world—as could be seen by their desire to pursue the retreating enemy. Then after a brief evocation of the virtues and triumph of the Gallican army, Marot evokes in a terrifying description the horrors of the Serpent, War. The petition is a moving call for peace (ll. 27–36), whereas the conclusion (ll. 36–55) expresses Marot's hope that Peace will return because of the cyclical nature of history: Peace engenders Prosperity, Prosperity leads to Wealth, Wealth to Pride and Pleasure, Pride to Contention, Contention to Wars, War to Poverty, Poverty to Humility, and Humility to Peace again. Marot closes with a prayer for peace.

This call for Peace as well as the matter-of-fact tone in which Marot reports the battle have led to reductionist interpretations that overlook the ethical hierarchies that structure Marot's epistles. Marot is seen really to want Peace while only paying lip service to war. Yet as the cycle Marot outlines indicates, there are times to expect war and times to hope for peace. The verse epistle is written in the expectation of war and enthusiastically describes the merits of the French army. The prose epistle is written in hope for peace after the battle is won. This kind of perspective that puts all experience in its proper place is also indicative of an elevated poetry. Lower-style poetry tends to emphasize partial experiences or the error of vices. Thus it is too easy to interpret Marot's style as an indication of flattery in a situation where there is nothing to say. We see the discrepancy between the humble style and the elevated content as the poet's attempt to convince his patroness that despite his humble origins—he is not a warrior—he is capable of dealing with serious matters.

The next two poems seem to be what Sebillet has in mind when he says that epistles about love that are not elegies are in a more popular style.[8] (They do not, however, have superscriptions and subscriptions.) Here suddenly after four formal poems, Marot shifts to a lighter mode of poetry. What we understand by "popular" is the way in which the love epistle defuses and distances feelings as opposed to the elegy which, we shall see, elaborates upon them. The group authorship of the "Epistle to a Maiden Negligent in coming to see her Friends" (*Epîtres,* IV) in itself takes the seriousness out of the situation. The friends playfully discuss different ways for the Maiden to come see them. Particularly light is the mixture of pedantic mythology (Pegasus), schoolish Latin ("Obsecro te," l. 28), with low-style words such as the diminutive "sautelle" (l. 17), and the allusions to the lower aspects of the horse's anatomy: the road *crotté* (littered with horse dung, l.27) or the allusion to holding the horse by its tail (l. 37). One has the impression of a schoolboy joke that Marot wrote in his adolescence. The epistle of the white garters (*Epîtres,* VII) contains a similar mixture of high and low in the very fact of the element of clothing it represents. Here Marot represents the playful beginning of a relationship (the maiden is an "ally," not yet a "friend") instead of the more entangled love of the elegies. Although he mentions *douleurs* (pains, l.7), he lightens the atmosphere with interrogations that lightheartedly mark the progress he would like to make from ally to friend to humble servant to deserving servant. The diminutives in the last two lines of the poem also cheer up the poem: "Si j'aime bien les blanches ceinturettes / J'aime encore mieux Dames qui sont brunettes" (If I like little white belts [i.e., garters] / I like Ladies who are brunette even better). These two poems and Maguelonne's epistle, therefore, show us that Sebillet's definition of the love epistle that is not an elegy actually refers to two different forms. Maguelonne's epistle is a long, formal poem about love with a subscription and recalls the *Heroides.* The other two epistles are lighter, popular poems about love that downplay sorrow and suffering.

## Epistles Written to Men

The epistles written to men are all of the lighter vein and playfully turn formal devices to comic purposes. The little epistle to the king

(*Epîtres*, I) makes fun with the kind of elaborate Rhétoriqueur prosody that Marot uses for serious ends in the epistle of the Destitute One. Marot writes to his sovereign a poem entirely made up of *vers équivoqués*—puns at the rhyme—in which the word *rhyme* itself is the center of the fun:

> En m'ébatant je fais Rondeaux en rime,
> Et en rimant bien souvent je m'enrime;
> Bref, c'est pitié d'entre nous Rimailleurs,
> Car vous trouvez assez de rime [*sic*] ailleurs.
>
> (ll. 1–4)

(While playing I make Rondeaux in rhyme / And in rhyming often I get all tangled up in rhymes [catch a cold]; / In brief, it is a pity among us rhymers / Because you find enough rhyme elsewhere.)

The poem is a joke but one of considerable virtuosity and has the serious purpose of winning patronage.

The following two poems in the *Adolescence* (*Epîtres*, V and VI) are satirical pieces. The first is written by Bourgeon (Bud) to Lord Rock for a horse. The second is written by an older, wiser Bourgeon now having become a Grape (Raisin) who describes how he got drunk, made love, and caught syphilis. Here it is the divergence between the elevated station of the persons and the low subject matter that is at the heart of the comedy.

The next two poems were written while Marot was in prison. They are in a plainer style as is appropriate for the class of persons they address. Yet their virtuosity exists in the density of meaning they generate despite their apparent transparence. They belong to a long tradition in which the plain style becomes obscure because it contains gaps and silences that are clear only to an author's intended audience.[9]

**The epistle to Bouchard, doctor of theology.** This poem (*Epîtres*, IX) is the most controversial of the epistles in the *Adolescence*. It is one of Marot's three main declarations of faith, along with "Hell" and the great epistle to Francis I from Ferrara.

In the exordium (ll. 1–9), Marot demands to know why Bouchard threw him—a friend—in prison for Lutheranism and then utters his famous declaration of faith. Quoted below is the 1538 version with a 1534 variant in brackets:

> Tiens de Luther? Point ne suis Luthériste
> Ni Zwinglien, & moins Anabaptiste [Papiste]
> Je suis de Dieu par son fils Jésus Christ.
>
> (ll. 7–9)

(I am neither Lutheran / Nor Zwinglian, and even less Anabaptist [Papist] / I am of God by his son Jesus Christ.)

In the narration (ll. 10–22), Marot defends his record as an orthodox writer in similarly vague terms. He says that he has not written a single line contrary to divine law (l. 12); that he praises Christ and His Mother (ll. 13–16); that he honors the holy, true, and Catholic church and no other doctrine (ll. 17–19). He concludes the narration by repeating that his law is good and that he prizes and exalts it (ll. 20–22).

The petition (ll. 23–38) is made up of several questions. Marot asks what Bouchard is looking for (ll. 23–24). He wishes that Bouchard would refrain from his mistaken anger (ll. 27–29) and that he could read his heart (ll. 30–32). Finally he begs that Bouchard be his friend (ll. 33–34), but then adds with a touch of irony that if Bouchard cannot act for him he should act on behalf of his friends and free him (ll. 35–38):

> À tant me tais, cher Seigneur notre Maître,
> Te suppliant à ce coup ami m'être.
> Et si pour moi à raison tu n'es mis,
> Fais quelque chose au moins pour mes amis.
>
> (ll. 33–36)

(Until then [until the doctor can read in his heart] I am keeping quiet, dear Lord our Master, / Begging you for now to be my friend. / And if you cannot bring yourself to it for my sake, / Do something at least for my friends.)

This last request is particularly aggressive for it implies that Marot has friends that Bouchard would do well to keep in mind.[10] Scholars, however, have overlooked the relation between this veiled threat and Marot's vague declaration of faith. Marot's silences and omissions indicate an arrogant refusal to enter into discussion rather than a fearful prudence. For he knows that the outcome will be determined by his "friends," that is to say, those influential at court.

It is doubtless because of his scorn and confidence that Marot did not find it necessary to dress up his style with formal techniques or give a more elaborate defense. Indeed, the studied conversational informality of the poem is full of arrogance. Consider in particular the scornful alliteration "Docte Docteur," the ironic possessive in "dear Lord our Master," or the insolent interrogations, such as "Que quiers-tu donc, ô Docteur catholique? / Que quiers-tu donc?" (So what are you looking for oh Catholic Doctor? / So what are you looking for?, ll. 23–24.)

Rather than read this defense as a subtly coded declaration of membership in one sect or another as scholars usually do, we prefer to understand it as a flippant rejection of all parties. Marot takes a doctor of theology head-on and establishes himself as a court evangelist above all sects—among which he included even the papists in 1534. Yet he condemns none of them. Only in an early manuscript version is there a specific condemnation of Lutheranism as an error "en tant de lieux maudite, / Contraire à tous et à tous interdite" (cursed in so many places / Contrary to everyone and forbidden to everyone, ll. 7–8). Marot, however, probably never wrote this rejection, which violates the stance above all religious parties he so carefully maintains in "Hell," the printed versions of this epistle, and the epistle to Francis I from Ferrara. For as C.A. Mayer has shown, it also belongs to a manuscript in which several of Marot's poems have been arranged according to a Roman Catholic ideology.[11]

In this respect, Marot's defense is a manifestation of what A. Patterson calls a "hermeneutics of censorship" in a forthcoming study of seventeenth-century English writing. As she elaborately demonstrates, writers working in an atmosphere of censorship have a contract with power that allows them a certain amount of freedom as long as they do not go too far. Thus to protect themselves, they write open-ended texts about crucial matters which call attention to problems or indicate directions of thought, but cannot be decoded in one determinate manner. Such a way of writing is of course dictated by necessity, but it is not forcibly cynical, dishonest, or cowardly. As a member of the intellectual elite at court that was restlessly seeking reform and religious truth, Marot himself was not only following changes of opinion but influencing them as well. In the dynamic intellectual and political atmosphere of his times, he had both to protect himself against changes in court opinion as well as to accommodate his own potential for change and growth.

Like Marot, Ben Jonson, one of the major practitioners of Patterson's hermeneutics of censorship, was a master of the plain style as W. Trimpi has shown. As in Jonson's writings, Marot's silences

and omissions together with the conversational style suggest that
Marot expected his audience to understand him perfectly. This expectation is at least twofold. On the one hand, Marot's declaration
of religious faith probably appeals to basic evangelical convictions
that Marot held in common with his friends. On the other, Marot's
threatening arrogance is most likely an expression of the scorn he
also shared with his friends for those outside the royal fold. However,
the situation was volatile; religious and political opinions that were
safe one day became dangerously subversive the next. Marot's artful
silences instead of protecting, condemned him.

Indeed, historical circumstances suggest why he waited until 1534
to publish his arrogant silences. Marguerite's *Miroir de l'âme pécheresse,*
one of the more prominent works of court evangelism, was denounced for heresy by omission because she spoke of neither purgatory nor the saints. Some have also suggested that the true reason
for the condemnation may have been Marot's translation of Psalm
6 included at the end of the book. (Translation, let us recall, was
often a provocative act.) Be that as it may, in 1533 Francis I angrily
put down the Sorbonne's accusation of heresy by omission; he re-
quested the specific heretical passages in his sister's book. Since
there were none, the Sorbonne backed down.[12] The king's action
may well have amounted to a green light making safe for public
consumption the silence-filled defense that Marot had previously
reserved for the ears of the court. In any case, it most certainly
confirmed Marot's arrogant refusal to deal with the Sorbonne's doctors of theology. As we shall see in the chapter on Marot's religion,
however, shortly afterwards the situation radically changed.

**The Epistle to Lyon Jamet.**    The epistle to Lyon Jamet (*Epîtres,*
X) is the finest example of Marot's *élégant badinage* in the epistles
of the *Adolescence.* Rhétoriqueur formality is still apparent in some
of the rhymes and alliteration as well as the pun on Lyon Jamet's
name which is the excuse for the epistle—both men probably shared
a common training and delight for Rhétoriqueur wordplay. However, these are turned to humorous purpose as Marot creates a swift,
witty, conversational style to dress up an anguished cry for help.

The poem divides into prologue, narration, and petition. The
prologue (ll. 1–15) is an example of paralipsis—Marot lists the
subjects that he will not talk about: love, war, fortune, corruption,
God, and the women of Paris.

The narration (ll. 16–71) tells Aesop's fable of the lion and the rat. The lion saves the rat, and later the rat gnaws through the lion's trap.

The petition (l. 72) is very short. Marot draws the final implication, saying that if Lyon Jamet helps him, he will help Lyon. It follows so very naturally from the narrative that Marot need not dwell on his request. Indeed, the brevity of the petition is a major factor in this art of pleasant asking.

The poem is a masterpiece of the plain style—a term that includes Boileau's *élégant badinage*. The humorous plain style assumes that writer and audience share the same assumptions and worldview. This is evident in the prologue list of subjects Marot will not write about. It follows a tradition according to which a poet eliminates other types of poetry before announcing the genre he has chosen. Marot, however, adds a humorous dimension to the topos that underscores his relationship with Jamet as well as Jamet's wide-ranging expertise. He says, for example, "Je ne t'écris des dames de Paris, / Tu en sais plus que leurs propres maris" (I am not writing to you about the ladies of Paris, / You know more about them than their own husbands, ll. 10–11.)

The list of subjects also establishes Marot's stylistic level. In lines 1–10 he rejects forms of poetry that are traditionally in a more ornamented style. He says that he does not write of love, war, philosophy, abuses—the province of more highly ornamented satirical poems such as "Hell"—or religion. Lines 11–13 reflect the lower end of the spectrum: misogynist poetry about Parisian women, "rude" and "affable" poetry. Thus Marot's fable is in a plain style, but not a crude or grossly comic one.

In keeping with plain-style poetry, Marot's version of the fable is a masterpiece of wit and psychological realism. Especially striking is his way of lending human characteristics to animals: the ironic modesty of the rat, the stately pride of the lion. For example, he describes the rat's act of gratitude after the lion frees him as follows:

> [Il] mit à terre un genou gentiment
> Et, en ôtant son bonnet de la tête,
> A mercié mille fois la grand' Bête.
> (ll. 24–26)

([He] put his knee gently to the ground / And, removing his bonnet from his head, / Rendered a thousand thanks to the great Beast.)

Such irony recalls Marot's way of playing high against low styles. The mouse's noble gesture contrasts ironically with his humble position. Another example is the lion's expression of scorn at the rat's offer to help: "Va te cacher, que le Chat ne te voie!" (Go and hide so the Cat will not see you, l. 54). Here the irony comes from the contrast between the lion's exalted station and his familiar, conversational tone.

The contrast between the serious situation and the witty tone of the poem is another characteristic of Marot's plain style. It creates a deceptive simplicity that becomes very puzzling if we scratch the surface. For example, the rat was arrested for having "Mangé le lard & la chair toute crue." (Eaten lard and completely raw flesh, l. 19). This line has always been taken as a reference to the poet's having broken Lent, yet recent critics such as M. Screech have maintained that such is not the case because the line is based on the medieval colloquial expression, "manger le lard" ("eat pork fat") that means "to steal."[13] In fact, we are not really sure what Marot meant under this apparently clear, conversational mask if we try to fill in the silences. These silences, however, are not those of a romantic or modern poet trying to point to a private, ineffable domain; rather they are elliptical references that depend on a private vocabulary shared by the writer and his audience. This private vocabulary may well have suggested a religious philosophy to both Marot and Jamet as G. Defaux suggests.[14] However, such a possibility remains completely hidden to the modern reader. Far from religious, ironies and wit in the poem celebrate Marot's confidence in Jamet's power.

Many, including La Fontaine who wrote his own version of the fable, consider Marot's narrative too long; but Marot's poem is an allegory in which each detail corresponds to his own situation, whereas for La Fontaine, it is a psychological study and narrative in itself. Furthermore, although La Fontaine considerably shortened the fable, he uses many of Marot's devices elsewhere in his works.[15] Thus Marot's epistle stands as one of his early masterworks independent of his predecessors the Rhétoriqueurs and striking in its originality in relation to his successor, La Fontaine.

# Chapter Four

# "Complaints and Epitaphs"

The section "Complaintes et épitaphes," marks the first appearance of death poetry in the 1538 *Oeuvres*. All of Marot's death poetry presupposes the traditional tripartite rhetorical schema consisting of praise or blame of the deceased, lament, and consolation. (Molinet first introduced the latter topic into French.) Attendant topics to these are demonstration of loss and exhortation; the latter in Marot's poetry takes the form of a call to prayer. [1]

"Complaints and Epitaphs" creates a bridge between the epistles and the fixed forms. The complaints are the last of the long poems; the epitaphs are the first of the short ones. Although the poems within the section do not follow so strict an order as do the opuscules and the epistles, they all focus on feelings the survivors have about the dead. These range from bawdy laughter to a desire for reunion in the hereafter. The complaints and epitaphs contain some of Marot's most moving religious poetry. Like the biblical writers, Marot allows survivors to mourn their dead.

## The Complaints

The complaint is one of two long forms of death poetry in Marot's works; the other is the death elegy. The latter, as we shall see, features a narration of how a person died. The complaint, on the other hand, takes as its starting point the time after death and features the survivors' reactions. The complaint and elegy also belong to two different levels of style. Originally both genres come from the low style. The elegy, as we shall see below, belongs to a long tradition of ornamented low-style poetry. The complaint, however, has a more complex history. In Rhétoriqueur poetry it filled the role of formal funeral panegyric—hence the topic of consolation that Molinet introduced. Marot brings the genre back toward its original level. He scales down the genre considerably (around seventy lines as opposed to hundreds), uses Rhétoriqueur ornament with greater rigor and discretion, and refrains from extensive pathetic laments as did the Rhétoriqueurs.

Critics erroneously interpret the relatively limited space Marot attributes to lament as an indication of shallowness or of an optimistic (one might also add soul-numbing) Christian perspective. We must caution, however, that Marot's scaled-down laments give much more than superficial lip service to mourning. Marot never simply wipes away grief. Rather he pits lament against consolation, often allowing the two to stand in open contradiction. He always leaves behind unresolved dissonances of sorrow that, much more effectively and subtly than unwieldy Rhétoriqueur length, pay mourning its due.

The result is a more flowing lyric piece that in combination with the Rhétoriqueur ornament approaches a flowery middle style except for the mourners' unresolved sorrow. (The middle style's intent is to charm or conciliate.)[2] Yet the complaint too much recalls Rhétoriqueur formality to belong to the ornamented low style. It is in Marot's poetry a mixed-level genre in which the play between high and low authenticates human mourning. Marot, like biblical writers, acknowledges the reality of grief and tenderness. Even those who have a firm faith in the afterlife mourn their dead because they miss them. Intransigent mourning is the very essence of the *Adolescence* complaints. A serious form of Castiglione's "nonchalance," it breaks the rigid Rhétoriqueur mold that Marot inherited and constitutes a backdrop for the fine nuances of wit and humor in the plain-style epitaphs that follow in the 1538 edition. The aesthetic effect on a French Renaissance reader must have been somewhat like that of an impressionist formal portrait, which both recalls yet transgresses the limits of a stiffer genre. Religiously, the poems, along with the "Deploration for Florimond Robertet," are the deepest Marot ever wrote.

**The complaint for Malleville.** Critics usually devote only brief attention to the complaint for the Baron Malleville (*O.L.*, III) that begins the section. However, it functions as a reference point for the rest of the poems in the group because it clearly shows the intransigence of mourning central to the *Adolescence* genre. According to the title, the baron was a secretary to Marguerite with Marot and was killed during a campaign against the Turks. The poem combines lament and praise (ll. 1–59), offers a form of consolation (ll. 60–68), and closes with an exhortation to prayer (ll. 69–72). The lines devoted to lament and praise are made up of a series of addresses to Earth, Sea, Nature, Death, and Fortune. These personified abstractions outline what traditional cosmology called the sublunary realm of change as opposed to the permanence of the heavens. Marot inherited the idea of turning to them from George Chastellain's "La Mort du duc Philippe" and J. Robertet's "Complainte de la mort de George Chastellain." Although Marot's account is much shorter, it nevertheless communicates the poet's cosmic revolt at the death of his close friend. The address to Death and the exhortation are the most important parts in terms of the rest of the *Adolescence* group. In the address to Death, we see the mourner intransigently refuse to accept the consolations of Malleville's immortality through fame in this world or through grace in the next, on the grounds that Love obliges him to mourn. Speaking to death, he says of his friend:

> Quant est du corps, vrai est que meurtri l'as,
> Mais de son bruit, où jamais n'eut frivole,
> Malgré ton dard, par tout le Monde il vole,
> Toujours croissant, comme Lis qui fleuronne.
> Touchant son âme, immortelle couronne
> Lui a donné celui pour qui mourut;
> Mais quelque bien encore que Dieu lui donne,
> Je suis contraint par Amour, qui l'ordonne,
> Le regretter et maudire Beyrouth.
>
> (ll. 40–48)

(As for the body, it is true that you have murdered it, / But as for his reputation, in no way ever frivolous, / Despite your arrow, it flies throughout the World, / Always growing, like Lilies in bloom. / Concerning his Soul, an immortal crown / Has given him He for whom he died; / But whatever good thing that God may yet give him, / I am obliged by Love, who orders it, / To regret him and curse Beirut.)

This constitutes a rebuttal of Renaissance as well as medieval themes of consolation, for the theme of fame in this world is a reference to Petrarch's *Triumphs* that the Rhétoriqueurs introduced into French. In the consolation, Earth, Sea, Nature, Death, and Fortune give rather hard-hearted replies. They enunciate usual consolatory topics: Earth takes back what she produced; Death spares no one, Fortune is cruel. The poet, however, is not consoled. He bitterly turns away in a call to prayer:

> . . . supplions le fils de notre Dame
> Qu'en fin es Cieux il nous fasse voir l'âme
> Du feu Baron, dit Jean de Malleville.
>
> (ll. 70–72)

(. . . let us pray to the son of our Lady / That at the end in Heaven he lets us see the soul / Of the departed Baron, Jean de Malleville.)

Unrequited love turns Malleville's friends away from the cruel, impersonal, and changing sublunary realm to the prayerful desire that they will see Malleville's soul in Heaven. The mourners neither accept the sufferings of this life nor seek an immediate escape from them, but channel their grief into hope for consolation in the world to come.

Marot more clearly states the philosophy that justifies this approach to mourning in his 1530 epistle to Antoine de Lorraine (*Epîtres,* XXII). There he does not wipe away Lorraine's grief with religious consolation, but assigns to each its proper role. He says that it is appropriate to mourn, but in mourning we must turn our wills to God (ll. 25–36). Here as in the complaint, Marot suggests a sensitive religious understanding of death. Rather than condemn the survivors' feelings of loss, he gives them a place within a larger scheme of things.

**The niece's complaint.**   The niece in the complaint that follows the poem for Malleville, however, does not seem to have learned this lesson as she laments the death of her aunt, Jane Bonté (*O.L.,* VI). Unlike Malleville's prayerful mourners, she nihilistically calls for death as an end to her suffering. (See ll. 53–66.) Marot discreetly uses Rhétoriqueur personification, repetition, and wordplay to dramatize the niece's sorrow. Most noteworthy is the halting, sobbing rhythm he creates through *rime concatenée:* the repetition of the last line of each stanza as the first of the following stanza.

The two-line epitaph (*O.D.,* XC) that follows in the 1538 edition adds the heavenly perspective lacking in the niece's suicidal grief. In two brief lines Marot deftly assures that the aunt has gone straight to heaven: "Ci est le corps Jane Bonté bouté / L'esprit au Ciel est par bonté monté" (Here lies Jane Bonté's body / The spirit to Heaven has by goodness gone). The alliterations and repetitions in this brief epitaph administer a witty antidote to the niece's dark despair. Yet, if we follow the 1538 edition, we do not completely discount the niece's sorrow because we remember the more nuanced complaint for Malleville, where mourning neither sinks into such despair nor resolves into easy consolation. In fact the artful 1538 juxtaposition of the two complaints and the epitaph creates a provocative silence around the poems intentionally. The poet respects the sufferers' loss and shrugs at the power of philosophy to heal. He is asking the reader not merely to think about mourning, but to experience with the survivors the inadequacies of consolation in the face of painful loss. The epitaphs in the next section of the 1538 edition add still more nuance to Marot's position on mourning.

## Epitaphs

Marot's epitaphs are pieces supposedly—and often actually—written for tombstones. Marot always recalls their nature as inscriptions through some allusion—most often the formula *ci-gît* (here lies)—which implies the reader's presence at the dead person's resting place. J. Plattard has suggested some of Marot's epitaphs are too long to have been written on tombs.[3] Even the longest, however, are relatively short compared to Ronsard's epitaphs. They belong to a Renaissance tradition that comes from the *Greek Anthology* through Martial and neo-Latin poets such as Pontanus and Marullus. In particular, Marot takes over the most striking neo-Latin innovation, the practice of satirical epitaphs—jokes about the dead—which give good occasion for his elegant banter.

These epigrammatic poems—the epitaph, after all, is a funeral epigram—belong to the plain style par excellence. Their elliptical brevity presupposes knowledge of the rhetorical schema of death poetry: praise, demonstration of loss, lament, consolation, and exhortation, but they often feature only one of these elements or fuse many of them together in the concise wit of the short form. For example, the epitaph "De Longueil, homme docte" (*O.D.*, XCI) merely suggests the topic of lament in the word *deuil* (mourning) which rhymes with *Longueil*.

The poems in the *Adolescence* commemorate the people at the fringe of court life: wives of court functionaries, a humanist, a silversmith, a court doctor, a poet, secretaries, jesters, and fools, including the *basochien* Jean Serre. The style of these early epitaphs shows the influence of the Rhétoriqueurs in the rich rhyme and alliteration,

which, however, avoids excessive mechanics in keeping with Marot's
plain-style aesthetic. In the satirical epitaphs the rhymes drive home
comic effects. For example, Jean Levesque, the shoemaker, who was
bishop in name only, died of syphilis. Marot closes with the prayer,
"Prions Dieu qu'au frère Frappart / Il donne quelque chambre à
part" (Let us pray to God that to the brother Belly Bumper / He
gives a separate bedroom) (*O.D.*, XCVI, ll. 9–10).

The collection is a masterpiece of nuanced emotion of which we
can only give a few examples. In the epitaph for Longueil (*O.D.*,
XCI) the man's fame rightly acquired through learning is cutely
stood on its head so that it is a reason for lament rather than
consolation. In the following epitaph (*O.D.*, XCII), the value of
silversmith Paulmier d'Orleans is established, not through world-
wide fame, but through the regret of his friends. Here too the
notion of fame is called into question. In his way, the silversmith
has just as much merit as Longueil. The epitaph on the court
physician André le Voust evokes with quick irony the doctor's de-
caying body. We understand how good and beautiful Catherine
Budé was through her husband's tears. The wide range of feeling
in this section—especially when considered together with the two
complaints as Marot would have us do—shows that the elegant
banter of the epitaphs is not shallow, but looks away from the stiff
Renaissance and medieval consolations of fame and salvation to
concentrate on the very human reactions we have not only when
our friends but when our foolish neighbors die. Both the laughter
and the grief are expressions of love. Marot himself shows how closely
the two are linked in the epitaph for Jean Serre (*O.D.*, CIII), which
closes the 1538 collection. After a masterfully rapid evocation of
the powdered and befeathered actor, he shows the Parisians laughing
and crying at the same time:

> Que dis-je? on ne le pleure point?
> Si fait-on, & voici le point:
> On en rit si fort en maints lieux
> Que larmes viennent aux yeux.
> Ainsi en riant on le pleure,
> Et en pleurant on rit à l'heure.
>                                    (ll. 43–48)

(What am I saying? we do not weep for him? / Oh yes we do, & here
is the point: / We laugh so hard that in many places / Tears come to our

eyes. / Thus in laughing we weep for him, / And in weeping we laugh at the same time.)

Then in a single stroke he calls into doubt the ultimate value of the reactions he has been painting:

> Or pleurez, riez votre saoul!
> Tout cel' ne lui sert d'un sou.
> Vous feriez beaucoup mieux (en somme)
> De prier Dieu pour le pauvre homme.
>
> (ll. 49–52)

(Thus cry, laugh to your heart's solace! / All that's not worth to him a cent. / You'd do a lot better (on the other hand) / To be prayin' God for the poor man.)

Such a compassionate philosophy applies to all the mourners in the *Adolescence* collection. Our laughter, our mourning, are for the survivors, and Marot's complaints and epitaphs let the survivors laugh and cry to their heart's solace rather than offering them specious consolations. Here at the end, in a delicate resumption of distance, he nonchalantly reminds us before moving on to another genre that such reactions are absolutely useless to the dead. In this case, the distance functions as the silences that reigned in the spaces around the complaints earlier. The poet steadfastly refuses total emotional involvement for himself. He always steps back to observe. Out of affectionate respect for his subjects and resignation to the vicissitudes of life, he indulges the mourners tenderly and admonishes them lightly. Here we see a fleeting glimpse of the poet's fine balance of head and heart that makes the 1538 section, "Complaintes et épitaphes," one of Marot's greatest achievements. Without the slightest trace of sentimentality, the poet infuses the intellectual gymnastics he inherited from the Rhétoriqueurs with a great depth of human warmth and understanding.

# Chapter Five
# Ballades, Rondeaux, Chansons

The next three sections of the *Adolescence* contain strophic poems—ballades, rondeaux, and songs. There is a hierarchical logic in their order that is lost in the Mayer edition. In all probability the 1538 order reflects Marot's definitions of the three genres, which correspond to the conventional usage of his time. The ballades come first. They are longer and traditionally more serious poems, although, as Sebillet points out, by the sixteenth century poets adapted them to a lighter subject matter.[1] Traditionally, the rondeaux are of lesser import than the ballades. The songs, inspired by a French popular tradition, are the most relaxed. They have no fixed form. Their strophic structures are of varying shapes so as to respond to subtle shifts in mood and tone. Although seventeenth-century précieux writers such as Voiture and Malleville were to find Marot's fixed-form poetry quintessential to their inspiration, he himself would abandon it in his later years for the freer, more responsive epigram. On the other hand, he will retain, develop, and augment the flexible prosodic forms of the songs for his ground-breaking translations of the Hebrew psalms.

## Ballades

Attractive to generations of late medieval writers eager to display their technical virtuosity, the ballade—first standardized by Guillaume de Machaut—was on the decline among sixteenth-century French poets aspiring to redefine their craft according to lofty Italian Renaissance ideals of poetry. Marot wrote most of his ballades[2] before 1527 in the period of apprenticeship to his Rhétoriqueur father. The son cast them all in the same mold of three stanzas, ranging in length from seven to twelve lines, and an envoy, which is roughly half the length of the preceding stanzas. With the exception of Ballade II (*O.D.*, LXVIII), all of these poems are what Sebillet calls "unisones"—that is to say, the stanzas of each ballade are all constructed on the same rhyme schemes.[3] The ballades with eight-line stanzas are in octosyllables. The rest are in decasyllables. Of the nineteen ballades Marot wrote, fourteen, which range from uneven youthful attempts at formality to masterful comic statement, constitute a separate section of the 1538 *Adolescence*. The others, written after 1527, appear in the *Suite:* a delicate love poem among the elegies and four pieces of a mature, controlled formality in the *chants divers*.

A hierarchy of subject matter determines the arrangement of the *Adolescence* ballades. The first five poems deal with subjects traditionally belonging to the low style. Ballades I and II refer to student associations. We hesitate to call these poems examples of the plain style because they travesty formal high-style devices such as complicated syntax, allegorical capitalization, and learned mythological allusions. The plain style creates the impression of a more simply ornamented conversational wit.

In Ballade III (*O.D.*, LXIX), Brother Lubin, a drunkard, violates the vows of obedience, poverty, and chastity. This satire, the most original of Marot's ballades, innovates the double refrain. It also uses infinitives in a way that prefigures du Bellay's satirical sonnets on the papacy. Here is Marot's stanza devoted to chastity and drinking:

> Pour débaucher par un doux style
> Quelque fille de bon maintien
> Point ne faut de Vieille subtile
> Frère Lubin le fera bien.
> Il prêche en Théologien;
> Mais pour boire de belle eau claire,
> Faites la boire à votre Chien
> Frère Lubin ne le peut faire.
> (ll. 17–24)

(To debauch with a smooth line / Some proper girl / A subtle Old Woman you don't need / Brother Lubin will do it just fine / He preaches as a Theologian; / But to drink nice clear water / Go get your dog! / Brother Lubin can't do it.)

Traditionally satire is one of the domains of the plain style, but here Marot's creative imagination stretches the familiar boundaries so that the conversational inflections of the satirical plain-style voice play against as well as with the ballade's fixed framework of infinitives and refrains. The first half of the stanza begins with a formal vocabulary ("de bon maintien") and syntax—the inversion of the negative, l. 19, and the delay of the main verb until the first refrain. This careful structuring mockingly suggests the monk's sophisticated sweet talk as well as the narrator's controlled indignation. The second half of the stanza is more incisive with shorter syntactic units in which the satirist's anger finally barks out in the "Faites la boire à votre Chien." This interruption resolves the syntax with a main verb in the imperative before the refrain.

Marot also uses the formal Rhétoriqueur device of capitalization to satirical purpose since it puts the Old Woman—the long-winded Duenna of the *Romance of the Rose*—the Theologian, and the Dog on the same plane. Notice also that "Chien" rhymes with "Chrétien" of the first stanza.

Ballade V (*O.D.*, LXXI), in which Marot asks to be inscribed on the rolls of Marguerite's household, is also a low- rather than a plain-style poem because of Marot's elaborate play on the word *couché*, which means both "lying down" and "inscribed in the household":

> L'un soutient contre cinq ou six
> Qu'être accoudé c'est musardie!
> L'autre qu'il n'est que d'être assis
> Pour bien tenir chère hardie;
> L'autre dit que c'est mélodie
> D'un homme debout bien fiché.
> Mais quelque chose que l'on die, [dise]
> Il n'est que d'être bien couché.
>                                          (ll. 17–24)

(Some maintain against five or six / That to be on your elbows is a dream / Another that there's nothing like being seated / To have a hardy countenance; / Others say that it is the melody / Of a man firmly standing up. / But, whatever one says / There's nothing like being well bedded down.)

Marot originally wrote this ballade in 1528 to Jean de La Barre in hopes of gaining entry into the king's household. His change of addressee gives the impression that the poem was written years earlier in a campaign to win Marguerite's patronage. The lie helps to cultivate the impression of a chronological arrangement in the *Adolescence* ballades. It suggests that the period of Marot's carefree student days ended with his entry into Marguerite's household. Furthermore, the five following ballades (*O.D.*, LXXII–LXXVI), written during Marot's service to the princess, are in a higher style appropriate to an established courtier. For example, Ballade VII (*O.D.*, LXXIII), which celebrates the birth of Dauphin François, duke of Brittany in 1517, is an interesting early attempt at a neoclassical high style with its Latinized "Neptunus," Latin place and ethnic names such as "Gaul," and the epithet "ondes salées." However, capitalized words such as "Mer"—now in a serious setting— recall the formal use of the Rhétoriqueur ornament.

The collection ends with a series of ballades on the most elevated of subjects, religion, dealing with Christmas, Lent, and the Passion (*O.D.*, LXXVII–LXXIX). This group, however, presents a curious mixture of high and low styles that perhaps points to the spiritual world's transcendence over all earthly hierarchies. For example, Ballade XI (*O.D.*, LXXVII) on Christmas is a call to hope and joy but in the low style of the medieval pastoral tradition. Aside from the pastoral vocabulary, the rhymes in *ec, ac, ic, oc,* and *uc* set a humble tone appropriate to shepherds. Yet the references to the prophets Eli and Enoch as well as the allegory of the Child and the Cross mark the elevation of the subject matter. The poem belongs to a long tradition of Christmas pastorals. It illustrates the theme of the Son of God born in humble surroundings. Ending the series is the famous ballade "Contre celle qui fut s'Amie" (*O.D.*, LXXX) with its refrain, "Prenez le, il a mangé le lard" (Arrest him, he ate the fat). Here the low style is communicated mainly in the short octosyllabic verse line and in the low-class vocabulary that suggests thievery, vengeance, and lust. The refrain contains a medieval expression, *manger le lard,* meaning "to steal."

The place of this poem after Ballade XIII (*O.D.*, LXXIX) dealing with Christ's Passion has many functions. It suggests that the religious section was written about the time of Marot's first imprisonment and subtly identifies Marot with one of the thieves who were crucified with Jesus. Furthermore, the poem's place only two ballades after the one devoted to the fasting of Lent actualizes the literal meaning of the refrain expression to show that Marot was eating meat during Lent. Thus once again as in the poem to Marguerite, we see Marot subtly creating his legend.

The last poem of the group is the "Chant Royal de la Conception notre Dame" (Chant Royal on the Conception of our Lady). The Virgin Mary is the spiritual opposite of the lusty girlfriend who denounced the poet in the preceding poem just as Christ of the Passion ballade is the antithesis of the thieving poet. The prosodic structure of the poem, a double ballade, as well as the allegory that develops the image of the elegant royal pavilion is a poem unmistakably in the Rhétoriqueur high style. Yet there are nevertheless touches of humility in the mention of the camp bed (1. 9) and the references to the great Pastor and his sheep. Here as in the other religious poems, the spiritual reality transcends and confounds worldly hierarchies.

## Rondeaux

According to Thomas Sebillet, Marot's rondeaux[4] are youthful works written in imitation of his father, Jean.[5] Indeed, of the sixty-six rondeaux he wrote, fifty-six were written before 1527. In the beginning of Francis I's reign, the rondeau was the most popular short form at court, but was to be superseded by the sonnet and the epigram, both in Marot's works and in that of his contemporaries. Originally, it was a song that accompanied a medieval short dance, the *rond;* however, Sebillet understands the name as a reference to the return of the refrain[6] Although Machaut first systematized the forms in the fourteenth century, Marot used simpler, shorter forms inherited from his father. Jean Marot, as many other of the Rhétoriqueurs, had reduced the refrain from a possible maximum of several lines to a few words. Sebillet defines four types of rondeaux: triolet, simple, double, and parfait. Most of Marot's are rondeaux doubles, whose rhyme scheme is *aabba aabr aabbar* (*r* = refrain). He also wrote a scattering of rondeaux simples (*abba abr abbar*) and one rondeau parfait: the "Rondeau parfait à ses Amis après sa délivrance." In this poem there is no refrain. Instead, each stanza ends with a line from the first. Most of the time Marot writes in decasyllabic lines with an occasional poem in octosyllables.

Sixty-four of the sixty-six rondeaux that Marot wrote appear together in the 1538 edition. Of the two others, one[7] precedes the "Temple of Cupid," the other,[8] follows "Maguelonne's Epistle." These two concisely summarize, comment upon, or sketch out a development of the themes from the works they follow.

Like the ballades, the sixty-four rondeaux that appear in the 1538 edition fall into cycles, which in this case, however, are too vague and numerous to describe in any detail except for the conclusion. Rondeau LXIV. A joyful celebration of Marot's release from prison, its distinctive form as his only rondeau parfait strikes a note of closure much as does the chant royal at the end of the ballades.

**A plain style ideal.** Marot's rondeaux show a much narrower choice of styles than the ballades, even though they cover a much wider range of subject matter. While the ballade accommodates both high and low styles, the rondeau is a plain-style genre, the characteristics of which Marot explains in the introductory piece to his collection. There for the only time in all of his works, he describes his aesthetic ideals for a poetic genre:

> En un Rondeau, sur le commencement,
> Un vocatif comme maître Clément
> Ne peut faillir rentrer par Huis ou Porte
> Aux plus savants Poètes m'en rapporte
> Qui d'en user se gardent sagement.
>
> Bien inventer vous faut premièrement;
> L'invention déchiffrer proprement,
> Si que Raison & Rime ne soit [sic] morte
> En un Rondeau.
> Usez de mots reçus communément;
> Rien superflu n'y soit aucunement,
> Et de la fin quelque bon propos sorte.
> Clouez tout court; rentrez de bonne sorte!
> Maître passé serez certainement
> En un Rondeau.
>
> (O.D., I)

(In a Rondeau, at the beginning, / A vocative like Master Clement / Cannot help but enter by the gate or Door / I refer you to more learned Poets / Who wisely stay away from using it. / / First of all you have to invent well; / Then work out the invention properly, / So that Reason & Rhyme be not dead / In a Rondeau / Use commonly received words; / Let there be nothing superfluous, / And let something good come out of the end. / Nail things shut; shut the door! / You will certainly be a past master / In a Rondeau.)

It is apparent here that a plain style is not necessarily an easy one. One should use commonly received words (1. 10), but proper names are too easy to make into a refrain: they cannot fail to enter through the "door or gateway" (1. 3). Marot also speaks of mastery, skill, strict economy ("nothing superfluous," 1. 10), and rhetorical invention.

This opening rondeau is a good description of the rest of the poems in the collection. Not all the refrains create an effect of surprise as does, for example, "Qu'on mène au champs" (O.D., VII). Still, most refrains are quite skillfully managed. Refrains characterize the dominant idea or feeling: the emotions attendant to a day, "un mardi gras," or the nostalgia for another epoch of love, "au bon vieux temps" (in the good old days). They create delicate moods of lightheartedness, sentimentality, and melancholy, without, however, suggesting any metaphysical anguish.

The rondeaux also usually follow Rondeau I's plain-style ideal of natural speech. The refrains are often bits of conversation so that the popular tradition of the French song runs strongly beside learned conventions. Consider, for example, Rondeau XXXIX (O.D., XXXIX), addressed to damsels who have not written. It plays on everyday greetings such as *bonjour* and *bonsoir:*

> Bon jour, & puis, quelles nouvelles?
> N'en saurait-on de vous avoir?
> S'en brief ne m'en faites savoir,
> J'en ferai de toute nouvelles.
>
> Puis que vous êtes si rebelles:
> Bon Vêpre, bonne Nuit, bon Soir,
> Bon jour
> mais si vous cueillez des Groseilles,
> Envoyez m'en; car, pour tout voir,
> Je suis gros, mais c'est de vous voir
> Quelque matin, mes Demoiselles.
> Bon jour!

(Good day, & so, any news? / Can't we get any out of you? / If you don't send any soon, / I will make some up. / Since you are so stubborn: / Good Vespers, good Night, good Evening, / Good day! / But if you go picking gooseberries / Send me some; because, by the looks of it / I am bursting, but to see you / Some morning, my ladies. / Good day!)

The conversational tone and wit in this poem create a distance from the poet's feelings. We see Marot consciously using "Raison" to dominate varying emotions and put them in perspective. By this means, he brings an analytical quality to love poetry that is characteristic of what W. Trimpi calls "passionate plainness" and extends the domain of the plain style to more serious matters.

The plain style, with its intention to describe accurately the personal experience or real situations, brought to the English love poem, which had before been the property of the *genus floridum*, an intensity of feeling derived not only from the candid sincerity of the author's statement but also from the urbane evaluation of the position that any specific kind of love should hold in relation to the human context of his experience as a whole. In this sense, the style encouraged in the love poem that same critical awareness of human values and human situations which it had first brought to satire from its Socratic origins.[9]

This plain-style emphasis on urbanity and critical awareness is one of the main elements in Marot's creative way of imitating Petrarchan love poetry in the rondeaux. Marot's love poetry more often alludes to general conventions than to specific authors, but the rondeaux are something of an exception because they have more precise textual echoes than usual.

**Petrarchism in the rondeaux.** The most obvious Petrarchan conventions that past critics have noticed are antitheses,[10] the exchange of hearts, the distinction between heart and body, the wounds that the lover receives through the lady's eyes or mouth, the sweetness of the lady's breath, nature imagery and birds, the pleasant pain of love, the lover's solitude, and the theme of carpe diem (seize the day and enjoy youth).[11] These conventions, however, have ample precedent in medieval French poetry from the *trouvères* to Charles d'Orleans,[12] and it would be difficult to distinguish the courtliness of the rondeaux from their Petrarchism were it not for the fact that they, more than Marot's later verse, echo specific poems of Petrarch and Petrarchan writers such as Serafino and Tebaldeo.[13]

The matter is all the more delicate because we must read Marot's imitations through a plain-style filter. Consider, for example, Rondeau XLVI (*O.D.*, XLVI), which everyone considers to be an imitation of Petrarch's famous sonnet "Solo et pensoso . . ."[14]

Tout à part soi est mélancolieux
Le tien Servant, qui s'éloigne des lieux
Là où l'on veut chanter, dancer et rire.
Seul en sa chambre, il va ses pleurs écrire,
Et n'est possible à lui de faire mieux.

Car, quand il pleut, et le Soleil des Cieux
Ne reluit point, tout homme est soucieux,
Et toute Bête en son creux se retire
Tout à part soi.
Or maintenant pleut larmes de mes yeux.
Et toi qui es mon Soleil gracieux
M'as délaissé en l'ombre de martyre.
Pour ces raisons loin des autres me tire,
Que mon ennui ne leur soit ennuyeux,
Tout à part soi.[15]

Solo et pensoso i più deserti campi
vo mesurando a passi tardi et lenti,
et gli occhi porto per fuggire intenti
ove vestigio uman la rena stampi.

Altro schremo non trovo che mi scampi
dal manifesto accorger de le genti,
perché negli atti d'allegrezza spenti
di fuor si legge com'io dentro avampi.

Sì ch'io mi credo omai che monti et piagge
et fiumi et selve sappian di che tempre
sia la mia vita, ch'è celata altrui;

ma pur sì aspre vie né sì selvagge
cercar non so ch'Amor non venga sempre
ragionando con meco, et io con lui.[16]

The nature of the imitation seems remote and tenuous. Both
poems share the idea of solitude. The word *melancholy* is an adaptation
of *pensoso* common to Petrarchist poets who interpreted *pensoso* as a
medical disorder related to an excess of the black choler, or
melancholy.[17]

Some curious yet more viable relationships between the two poems
may show that Petrarch influenced Marot, but not in the generally
assumed way. Both poets use foot imagery and refer to reading and

writing. Petrarch goes about "with steps delaying and slow" (l. 2) and flees "from where any footprint marks the sand" (l. 3). Marot avoids places where people are dancing (l. 3). Furthermore, Petrarch withdraws so that people cannot "read" (l. 8) the passion that burns within him. Marot withdraws so as to "write" (l. 4) of his tears. However, it could be argued that even these parallels are incidental. In my view, the poems are entirely different in every other respect.

Marot brings a plain-style rationality and concern for society to Petrarch's experience. The lover in Petrarch's poem seeks solitude to hide his love from society (second quatrain). Marot is more "altruistic." He escapes not to hide from society's knowing glances but to spare others, who are singing, dancing, and laughing (l. 3), the annoyance of his own pain (l. 14). Marot's melancholy is also much less anguished than Petrarch's pensiveness. Petrarch seeks to escape from love itself (second tercet). Marot withdraws not to forget love but to write about it (l. 4—a standard means of poetic purification. Marot also maintains more of a distance from his melancholy than Petrarch because he considers it from a rationalistic perspective. He inscribes his feeling in networks of generalizations, social relationships, and the laws of nature. When the courtier suffers, he withdraws from the society to his bedroom. When it rains, wild animals retire to their caverns. Suffering itself is part of a natural cycle like that of sun and rain. One has the impression that it will pass in due time. The analogies to rain, sun, and the behavior of animals create an intellectualized level of ornamentation that is the serious counterpart to the witty conversational banter of the previously considered Rondeau XXXIX (*O.D., XXXIX*).

Furthermore, Petrarch uses metaphor as a structural device.[18] Here the lonely deserted pathless ways of open nature constitute a single metaphor from the beginning to the end of the sonnet. Metaphor in Marot's rondeau, on the other hand, does not have a structural function, but recalls French medieval lyric technique. Marot uses capitalization, but does not develop a coherent allegory. (Allegory, remember, was originally considered to be an extended metaphor.) Here the Sun is the lady but functions in two different structures.[19] The sun is hidden because it is raining (l. 6) and because it has temporarily disappeared—perhaps behind a tree—leaving the poet in the shadows (l. 12). Even the rain metaphor functions in two different ways. It is raining so the poet withdraws (ll. 6–9) and it is raining tears from his eyes.

Marot's ornamental use of metaphor, however, reflects a plain-style aesthetic in that it implies a set of universally accepted laws and analogies to which the poet can elliptically refer and still expect to be understood. References to sun, tears, rain, and shadow, as well as the use of capitalization, appeal to familiar, time-honored associations and usages in early sixteenth-century France.

One would call the Petrarchism of this poem pre-Petrarchan because of the limited, indirect nature of the imitation, the ornamental rather than structural use of metaphor, and the intellectual distance that Marot maintains from his passion. These differences, however, are also the very stuff of the kind of plain style that Marot consistently uses to create a lyric genre in which the mind dominates the heart.

Marot's shift from the rondeau to the epigram probably occurred because the devices and practices of the former were no longer accepted as a neutral discourse. The capitalization, the complicated verse structure, and to a lesser extent, the ornamental use of metaphor came to be felt as old-fashioned rather than familiar. After Marot, the Pléiade poets banished the rondeau from the poetic repertory. The form enjoyed a brief return to favor among the *précieux* poets such as Voiture, who fled classical plainness for the closed elitist ideal of the salon rather than the universalist elitism of the court.

## Chansons

Marot's songs come after the ballades and the rondeaux because they are freer—yet subtle—lyric pieces rather than intellectual feats of poetic skill. Gone are the demanding fixed forms of the ballades and rondeaux. The songs have no refrain—with one or two exceptions—and follow a rich variety of rhythm, meter, and versification that corresponds to subtle shifts in meaning and tone.

Sebillet considers the ode and song as the same—after all, *ode* is derived from the Greek word meaning "song."[20] The Pléiade, of course, had much greater designs for the ode. However, some of the Pléiade's lighter odes resemble Marot's songs, and it is Marot and not Ronsard of the odes who restored French lyric poetry—in the proper sense of poetry written to be sung—to serious literature. The Rhétoriqueur's verbal and prosodic acrobatics had gone so far that even rondeaux and ballades could no longer be set to music.[21]

Marot's songs begin an experimentation with a variety of forms that was to culminate in his translation of the psalms, which in turn provided the prosodic models for Ronsard's odes. In poets of the plain style such as Catullus, Martial, and Ben Jonson, it is often difficult to distinguish between amatory epigrams and songs. Marot's songs,[22] however, can be distinguished from the epigrams and the rondeaux because they do not have the necessary wit and urbanity. They are in a low style that cannot be called plain in the usual sense of the term. Rather they are in an elegant low style whose simplicity is a refined version of the fifteenth-century popular song tradition. Here we see one of Marot's most creative poetic accomplishments. The opening piece of the collection is a striking contrast to the intellectual theorizing that begins the rondeaux:

> Plaisir n'ai plus, mais vis en déconfort,
> Fortune m'a remis en grand' douleur;
> L'heur que j'avais est tourné en malheur,
> Malheureux est qui n'a aucun confort.
>
> Fort suis dolent & regret me remord,
> Mort m'a ôté ma Dame de valeur,
> L'heur que j'avais est tourné en malheur,
> Malheureux est qui n'a aucun confort.
>
> Valoir ne puis, en ce Monde suis mort,
> Morte est m'amour, dont suis en grand langueur,
> Langoureux suis, plein d'amère liqueur,
> Le coeur me part pour sa dolente mort.
>
> (*O.L.*, X)

(Pleasure have I no longer, but live in discomfort, / Fortune has thrown me back into great pain; / The happiness I had has turned to unhappiness, / Unhappy the one who has no comfort. / I am in great pain and regret gnaws at me, / Death has taken away my Lady of great value, / The happiness that I had has turned to unhappiness, / Unhappy the one who has no comfort. / I am good for nothing, dead to this World, / Dead is my beloved, I languish away / Languishing am I, full of bitter liquor, / My heart leaves me for its painful death.)

Here there is no longer any intellectual distancing of passion but a direct lyric cry of suffering. "Bitter liquor" is a reference to the

melancholy, or black choler, of the rondeau, but the medical terminology is more sustained in the song with such words as *discomfort,*
*pain,* and *languishing.* The use of these words to paint a picture from
the vantage point of feelings rather than intellect is characteristic
of fifteenth- and early sixteenth-century popular songs.[23] Indeed,
Marot includes many of their incipits as lines in his own poems.
To the Renaissance reader, Marot's use of convention doubtless
recalled a free, direct, popular tradition that saw love uniquely in
terms of the heart in contrast to the more courtly rationalistic writing
characteristic of the rondeau.

Marot raises the level of the popular song, however, to an appropriate standard for court ears mainly through a skillful use of
prosody. Notice how the prosody of the poem artfully expresses the
shifts in the poet's passion. The poet's broken heart blocks the return
of the refrain in the last stanza. Furthermore, the repetitions of the
rhymes in the first words of the following lines creates a sobbing,
obsessive rhythm. It is as if the poet is suffering too much to set
forth a rational argument. He seizes rather on the immediate associations of words at hand.

The following song is like the rondeau based on daily greetings.
It is for a woman who has not written to the poet:

> Languir me fais sans t'avoir offensée,
> Plus ne m'écris, plus de moi ne t'enquiers,
> Mais nonobstant autre Dame ne quiers;
> Plutôt mourir que changer ma pensée.
>
> Je ne dis pas t'amour être effacée
> Mais je me plains de l'ennui que j'acquiers,
> Et loin de toi humblement te requiers
> Que loin de moi, de moi ne sois fachée.
>
> (*O.L.,* XXII)

(You make me languish without my having offended you, / No longer
do you write to me, no longer do you ask about me, / But nevertheless I
will not look for another Lady; / I would rather die than change my
thought. / I do not say your love to have been wiped away / But I complain
of the weariness that I acquire, / And far from you humbly beseech you
/ That far from me, you not be angry with me.)

Gone is the distancing wit of the rondeau. Instead of to several
ladies, Marot is writing to one who makes him suffer. As in the

preceding song, but in contrast to the rondeaux, there is a great density of words denoting feelings and emotions: *languish, offend, complain, ennui, humbly, angered.* The argument of the poem is simple and suggestive and recalls Fabri's tripartite schema for the "lettre d'amour vicieuse": praise of the lady, praise of the lover, and request. In fleeting rapid strokes Marot uses the theme of the lady's silence to sketch out praise of the lover (his constancy, innocence, and suffering), praise of the lady (no one else can compare to her, her love remains true) and a request not to be angry. The paralipsis of line 8—the poet does not say that the lady's love is gone—is particularly suggestive and delicate. That he dare not accuse her suggests both that she is too good for such a base feeling and that he fears the worst.

It is because past critics have overlooked the suggestive, emotional perspective of these songs that they have had difficulty in defining the genre. For example, V.L. Saulnier maintains that some of the epigrams are indistinguishable from the songs.[24] Yet, we shall see below that Marot's epigrams share the intellectual plain-style perspective of the rondeaux rather than the emotional point of view of the songs.

Aside from the ease, simplicity, and lightness of these songs, it is often difficult to identify precise elements from the popular tradition. The troubadours, who founded the courtly conventions, wrote the songs that created the popular tradition as well. Furthermore, as time went on, writers in the lighter vein took over courtly conventions, much as American square dances reflected more formal European counterparts. Very few of Marot's songs employ clearly popular elements. Song XXV (*O.L.*, XXXIV) is a noel: a song in which different persons—notably shepherds—file past the manger. In Marot's poem, however, the shepherds simply call to sing of Christmas. Song XXXII (*O.L.*, XLI) is a bachique song, and songs XXIV, XXXVI, and XXXVIII (*O.L.*, XXXIII, XLV, XLVII) employ themes from bawdier, fabliau-type literature. They deal with humorous references to sexual acts, tricks played on husbands, and money. Song XXXIII (*O.L.*, XLII) is neither popular nor courtly. It simply repeats Venus's promise to Paris during his judgment between Venus, Minerva, and Juno that led to the Trojan War.

The rest of the songs incorporate courtly motifs as they came down from the troubadours and *trouvères* through the *Romance of the*

*Rose* and the fourteenth- and fifteenth-century poems in the *Jardin de Plaisance*. However, since such conventions are seen from the heart's point of view rather than the mind's, they are never really worked out. Marot makes only fleeting references to them much as he does in the plain-style rondeaux. But there one has the impression that he alludes to commonly understood language, whereas here the suggestive quality implies a lover whose intense emotions make him incapable of greater elaboration.

Because these poems are so suggestive, it is impossible to identify precise women for whom they were written and thus reconstitute a coherent love story. J. Rollin has recently attempted to define cycles of poems much as those we have seen in the rondeaux and ballades.[25] Certain of the poems do answer each other or play on a single word such as *Jouissance* or treat a common theme. Yet they constitute even looser cycles than the rondeaux. The overall effect is that of a series of fleeting, incompletely articulated feelings that correspond to the impressionistically suggestive discourse of the genre.

## Chapter Six

# Two Formal Styles of Funeral Poetry, Marot's Eclogues

## Formal Funeral Poetry

The *Suite de l'adolescence clémentine* begins with two long funeral poems, "La Déploration de Florimond Robertet" ("Deploration for Florimond Robertet") and the "Eclogue sur le Trépas de ma Dame Louise de Savoie" ("Eclogue on the Death of Madame Louise de Savoie"). The 1538 table of contents classifies them as complaints—doubtless the reason that Sebillet calls the former a complaint in the form of a deploration and the latter a complaint in the form of an eclogue.[1] They are, however, much more fully developed than the *Adolescence* complaints; although they feature survivors' reactions in conformity to the genre, they represent different approaches to the relationship between lament and consolation. The deploration portrays intransigent mourning like the earlier complaints, but the eclogue contains a sudden shift from lament to consolation. Furthermore, the two poems are showpieces that represent entirely different styles of death poetry: the first is a full-scale Rhétoriqueur funeral deploration, the second is a pastoral elegy in the Italian Renaissance manner. This contrast as well as the opuscule-like dimensions of the poems justifies their place at the beginning of the *Suite.*

**"The Deploration for Florimond Robertet."** "The Deploration for Florimond Robertet" (*O.L.,* VI) is Marot's most overtly religious poem except for his last poems, which are of doubtful authenticity. It is an allegorical narrative of Florimond Robertet's funeral that follows the topics of death oratory: prologue, lament (which includes praise), consolation, and epilogue.

The prologue (ll. 1–172) announces the genre of the poem with a play on the distinction between love and death poetry. Marot says that love, not death, prompts him to write and that this love, not outward manifestations of mourning, is the true source of heartfelt grief. The rest of the prologue introduces the funeral procession. The poet sees hideous Death (not capitalized in Marot's text) triumphant in her chariot; a fairy (the Roman church, Dame Romaine) who hides her elegant trappings under a humble mantle; another woman, Françoise République; Labor; and finally, the casket. This section also includes praises of Robertet as the man who trained a corps of state secretaries to write.

The lament (ll. 173–284) is a long reproach that Françoise République addresses to Death. It also includes praises that emphasize Robertet's role as a beloved and esteemed councillor and man of letters. The author (*l'acteur*) announces the consolation—Death's rebuttal to Françoise République—which he characterizes as "a very useful and certain thing" (l. 284).

Death's consolation (ll. 285–452) is quite long and deserves detailed summary. She reproaches and jeers at the mourners: "Why do you have funeral ceremonies," she asks, "if you hate me? The priests who collect the money do not think I am so bad." She points out that funerals are more for the living than for the dead and that only the blood of Christ can wash the soul. She embarks on a long development showing that she is actually blessed because, thanks to Christ's sacrifice on the cross, she ends this woeful, treacherous life on earth and serves as a gateway to heaven. She attacks the deluded self-love that makes us hate her and want to go on living in this world. She counsels the mourners to pray for faith and hope in God and to be ready to suffer and leave all for Him. She brands the mourners' tears as hypocritical and against the will of God. For her, masses and death anniversaries are beautiful except for the avarice of the clergy who collects money for them; tombs are useless for salvation. Death summarizes the speech in recalling that to see God one must die and that at the very worst she takes us from the woes and worries of this world.

In the epilogue (ll. 453–555), the mourners refuse to listen to Death, who falls silent. As they continue the procession, all of nature recoils in horror at the sight of Death—a version of the world-upside-down topos that is conventional in funeral poetry. The mourners finally reach Blois where, despite Death's counsel, they hold a full funeral service, pray for Robertet's soul, and tearfully bury him.

The poem is a good example of a Medieval mixed formal style. The opening lines of Marot's prologue clearly raise the issue of stylistic level. He used to sing love songs (perhaps the songs we have just considered in the preceding chapter) in the low style:

> Jadis ma plume on vit son vol étendre
> Au gré d'amours, et d'un bas style et tendre
> Distiller dits que soulais mettre en chant.
>
> (ll. 1–3)

(Formerly my pen saw its flight extend / According to the wants of love, and of a low and tender style / Distill sayings that I used to put into song.)

But now because of regret he must go against his Muse's native bent ("le naïf de ma Muse," l. 29) that would not have him "compose in a sad tragic vein" ("composer en triste tragédie," l. 31). He must say a "song of death in a style full of distress" ("Chanson mortelle en style plein d'émoi," l. 33). The oppositions here are "low" versus the traditionally high "tragic," and "tender" versus "full of distress."

Marot, however, understands these terms like the Rhétoriqueurs rather than Ronsard and the Pléiade. The reference to "sayings," for example, recalls a Rhétoriqueur genre. In the rest of the poem, elevation is communicated through amplification in the medieval and Rhétoriqueur sense of lengthening instead of heightening. The personified abstractions of the poems also belong to Rhétoriqueur precedents—in this case, Jean Lemaire's "Plainte du désiré." And they mark the last appearance of such allegory in Marot's work except for the elegies and the complaint for Preudhomme, which in 1543 constituted something of a literary archaism.[2]

Furthermore, the tableau of Death triumphant recalls Petrarch's *Triumphs* as do the references to Robertet's fame. (The *Triumphs*, let us recall, came into French through the Rhétoriqueurs.) The contrast between the stanzas of the main body and the rhymed couplets of the prologue and epilogue is also a characteristic sign of Rhétoriqueur loftiness. When the characters such as Françoise République or Death speak, the stanzas give rise to stately oratorical argument and passion. Yet Marot never consistently sustains high-style oratory. The didactic content of Death's speech, for example, is a characteristic of the plain style, which, according to Quintilian, is most appropriate for instruction.[3] Elsewhere, the kind of ornamentation Marot uses will later in the French Renaissance be more characteristic of the mannerist or baroque middle style rather than the neoclassical high style. The following lines are an example of baroque or mannerist development of metaphor to unusual extremes:

> De vos deux yeux, vous, sa chère épousée,
> Faites fontaine ou puiser puisse eau!
> Filles de lui, votre face arrosée
> De larmes soit, non comme de rosée,
> Mais chacun oeil soit un petit ruisseau
> Chacun des miens en jette plus d'un seau;
> De tout cela faisons une rivière
> Pour y noyer la mort qui est si fière.
>
> (ll. 237–44)

(With your two eyes, you, his darling spouse, / Make a fountain where one can draw water / His daughters! May your face be bathed / In tears, not like dew, / But let each eye be a little brook / Each one of mine throw more than a bucket; / With all that let us make a river / To drown in it death who is so proud.)

Here the alliteration and development of the metaphor is doubtless a sign of middle-style floridness—remember the tears in the Beroaldus translation. At the same time, the low-style realistic evocations of drawing water from a well and the eyes throwing in more than a bucket of tears would disqualify this passage from a stricter neoclassical high style. These gestures, however, very touchingly communicate the distress Françoise République shares with Robertet's family. Other such touches of realism exist throughout the poem. For example, in the very moving passage that describes Death's effects as she moves through town and country, we see the people flee the town as she arrives. When she leaves however,

> . . . lors on épand et rue
> Eaux de senteurs & vinaigre en la rue.
> Puis es quentons feu de genièvre allument
> Et leurs maisons éventent & parfument
> À leur pouvoir de la ville chassant
> L'air que la mort y a mis en passant.
>
> (ll. 492–96)

(. . .then they spread out and pour / Perfumed waters and vinegar in the street. / Then in the public places they light fires of juniper / And air out and perfume their houses / Doing all in their power to drive out from the town / The air that Death left there in passing.)

The following stanza is closer to later neoclassical ideals doubtless because it evokes the epic contrast between warlike courage and wisdom. Françoise République says:

> Ha, la méchante! écoutez sa malice!
> Premier occit, en martial détroit,
> Quatre meilleurs chevaliers de ma lice:
> Lescut, Bayard, La Trémoille et Palice.
> Puis est entrée en mon conseil étroit,
> Et de la troupe alla frapper tout droit
> Le mieux aimé & le plus diligent.
> Souvent de tels est un peuple indigent.
> (ll. 245–52)

(Ah, the foul one! listen to her malice! / First she killed, in martial straits, / Four of the best knights of my command: / Lescut, Bayard, La Trémoille and Palice. / Then she came into my inner council, / And of the troop struck at the heart / The best loved and the most diligent. / Often of such a one is a people indigent.)

Here the apostrophes of line 245, the elevated vocabulary such as "occit" (l. 246) and "troupe" (l. 250), and the sententious maxim that concludes the stanza are all characteristics of the neoclassical elevated style. The combination of such techniques with Marot's realism is a sign of neither weakness nor ignorance. Rather it plays low against high so as to give a human dimension to the mourning. It is like the deliberately out of place realistic scenes carved on the capitals of columns in stately Gothic cathedrals.

Scholars have tried to find evidence of Marot's religious leanings toward Luther and other reformers in the allegorical portrait of the Roman Catholic church and in Death's speech (ll. 285–452), but C. Martineau-Génieys's recent demonstration of the affinities between these passages and Briçonnet's consolatory letters to Marguerite forces a sweeping reassessment.[4] Briçonnet, while an evangelist, was committed to reform within the Roman Catholic fold. Likewise, "The Deploration for Florimond Robertet" criticizes the church from within. In Death's speech, take, for example, the lines, "Prie à Dieu seul que par grace te donne / La vive foi dont saint Paul tant écrit" (Pray to God alone that through grace He gives / The living faith that Saint Paul wrote so much about, ll. 325–26). These lines have been taken to imply the Lutheran doctrine of justification by faith alone. Yet the expression *vive foi* ("living faith") is an allusion to James 2:17, "So faith by itself; if it has no works is dead."[5] Instead of opposing faith and works, Death opposes faith and empty funeral ceremonies. She is not against ceremony in itself. She says, "Messes sans nombre & force anniversaires / C'est belle chose" (Masses without number and many anniversaries / Are a beautiful thing, ll. 421–422). But she also recalls that they are often a function of priestly avarice and hypocrisy. Thus rather than make of Marot a secret Lutheran or adept of the sermoner Thomas Malingre,[6] we see Marot as a follower of the evangelism he learned from Marguerite and Briçonnet at a royal court that saw itself as a guarantor of the faith and an instrument of reform without a break from Rome. Just as the court is Marot's "schoolmistress" in matters of language, it is also his director of conscience.

Moreover, no one has considered the fundamental irony of the poem: a hideous, hated Death consoles with evangelistic doctrine. Nor has anyone considered how death's speech enters into the complaint's opposition between lament and consolation. C. Martineau-Génieys has observed that it is impossible to identify Marot with either Death or the mourners, but then interprets the people's refusal to hear Death's speech as a deafness to evangelistic doctrine.[7] Her explanation is more satisfying than that of M. Richter, who considers the portrayal of the disconsolate mourners as the superficial attempt to save the complaint form from the undermining effects of Death's theology of mourning.[8] The disconsolate grieving of the poem, however, is not a superficial formality. We have already seen in the complaint for Baron Malleville that the poet specifically rejects the consolation of arguments concerning fame or eternal salvation and mourns out of love. "The Deploration for Florimond Robertet" does likewise. The poet says that it is not death but love that spurs him away from love poetry and forces him to dip his pen into the "ink of bitterness" ("l'encre d'amertume," l. 6). Then he continues:

> . . . Car quand chacun mourrait,
> Sans vrai amour plaindre on ne le pourrait.
> Mais, quand la mort a fait son maléfice,
> Amour adonc [*sic*] use de son office,
> Faisant porter aux vrais amis le deuil,
> Non point un deuil de feintes larmes d'oeil,
> Non point un deuil de drap noir annuel,
> Mais un deuil teint d'ennui perpétuel;
> Non point un deuil qui dehors apparoit [apparaît],
> Mais qui au coeur sans apparence croît.
> Voilà le deuil qui a vaincu ma joie.
>
>                                    (ll. 13–23)

(. . .Because when each dies / Without true love, one cannot weep for him. / But, when death has done her dark deed, / Love then uses its offices, / Making true friends wear mourning, / Not a mourning of fake tears in the eyes, / Not a mourning wearing black for a year, / But a mourning tinted with perpetual emptiness, / Not a mourning that appears on the outside / But that grows in the heart invisibly. / That is the mourning that has conquered my joy.)

The death of a loved one leaves an emptiness in the heart that causes us to mourn our loss regardless of the fame or salvation of the departed. Françoise République picks up this theme of the loss that Robertet's death represents in her speech (see especially ll. 229–36 and ll. 245–52).

Death, however, does not address the question of the mourners' loss. She sees only another kind of love, a foolish self-love that makes us want to live: "Que dis-je aimer? Celui ne s'aime en rien, / Lequel voudrait toujours vivre en ce monde" (Do I say love? He does not love himself in any way / Who would wish always to live in this world, ll. 309–10). In a word, rather than console them for their loss, Death tells the mourners why they should accept her for themselves in the grand scheme of things. Thus there is indeed, as they say in French, a dialogue between people who do not hear each other. Death thinks the people mourn because they resist her themselves, but the people mourn out of love. The inhabitants of Blois where Robertet is to be buried do not flee Death as did other city dwellers: "Car du defunt ont plus d'amour empreinte / Dedans leurs coeurs que de la mort n'ont crainte" (Because for the departed they have more love planted / In their hearts than they have fear of Death, ll. 519–20). Rather than attempt to fill in the silence and decide whose side the poet is really on, it is better to allow for the openness of this text. Marot validates both Death's arguments and the mourners at once in a contradictory irony much like his declaration of faith in the epistle to Bouchard. Here, however, he does not simply banter with the wrath of the literary censors of his day. He gives support to the mourners in the prologue and epilogue passages on love, and support to death's speech in the acknowledgment that it is "useful and very certain" ("utile & très certaine," l. 284). Death is correct in terms of the mind, the mourners in terms of the heart.

Marot expresses a delicate religious sensitivity in "The Deploration for Florimond Robertet," not because of the long passages he devotes to doctrine, but rather because of the distance and irony he creates in relation to that doctrine. Here as in "Complaints and Epitaphs," Marot blesses those who mourn. Such a blessing resembles Marot's consolation in the 1530 epistle to Antoine de Lorraine (*Epîtres*, XXII), which we have discussed above. It is much more life affirming than a blissful acceptance of death because it accepts the contradictory nature which is the lot of all humanity. Even those who believe in an afterlife experience the loss of loved ones. Here as in "Complaints and Epitaphs," Marot achieves unusual human and religious depth that recalls the many mourners in the Bible.

**The Eclogue for Louise de Savoie.**   In this light, the eclogue for Louise de Savoie (*O.L.*, LXXXVII)—which follows the deploration in the 1538 edition—rings hollow, despite the fact that it is the first pastoral elegy in French. Gone is the uneasy tension between doctrine and heart, mourning and consolation. The "wound of love" is consoled and healed as the shepherd Colin turns abruptly away from sorrow to sing a song of rejoicing: "c'est assez déploré; / Elle est aux champs Elyséens reçue" (Enough of mourning / She has been received in the Elysian fields, ll. 190–91). In this, Marot follows Virgil's Fifth Eclogue which first juxtaposed songs of mourning and rejoicing in the funeral elegy, and like Virgil, he shifts the emphasis from mourning to praise, in singing of the queen mother's accomplishments.[9] Either Marot sacrificed the medieval complaint's subtle complexity to Virgilian convention, or he wrote these lines of easy consolation ironically. We shall consider both possibilities.

The poem consists of a prologue, a lament that also praises the queen mother, a consolation, and an epilogue. In the prologue (ll. 1–48), the shepherd Thenot promises the shepherd Colin a payment of six yellow and six green quinces for "dix fois dix Vers / En déplorant la Bergère Louise" (ten times ten Verses / Mourning the Shepherdess Louise, ll. 33–34), and even more if his song is better. Colin calls all shepherds to mourn in the lament (ll. 49–189). He first takes note of the king's sorrow and recalls how Louise trained the daughters of the nobility who came to live with her. He shows how the daughters wept along with the winds, plants, sun, sky, king (the great Shepherd), Marguerite, earth, sea, fishes, and animals (except wolves), and birds. Then he returns to the shepherds and calls them to approach the casket. He decries death for having taken away the woman who had so well protected France and lists a catalog of French cities that mourn Louise. He ends the catalog with an evocation of white swans singing. He calls the woodland fauna to awake and mourn. Then he asks why a person in a tomb never returns as do the grasses of the fields in the summer and remembers that a few days previous, the call of a crow in an oak tree had warned him that something ill was afoot in the realm.

Colin invokes his verses to sing of pain in the first line of the consolation (ll. 190–260), but then abruptly calls them to silence, paints a tableau of the Elysian fields where Louise has gone, calls the Savoisien nymphs to put flowers on the tomb of the shepherdess of Peace, invokes Pan to sing with greater grace than his poor poetry, and asks for his promised recompense.

In the epilogue (ll. 261–76), Thenot compliments Colin on his song, gives him more than he promised, and adjourns with the coming of night.

The eclogue's neoclassical style stands in marked contrast with the deploration's late medieval manner. A reflection of the new Italianism at the court around 1530, the poem echos Sannazaro and Luigi Alamanni. It also incorporates classical sources such as Theocritus's Idyll I and Moschus's funeral song in honor of Bion—even though Marot did not read Greek—as well as Virgil's Fifth Eclogue. Marot's borrowings are too numerous to list here. Any of the standard critical editions contain full documentation.

Besides the Virgilian juxtaposition of mourning and rejoicing, other pastoral conventions include the prologue's call to song with hints of a singing contest, and the variants of the line "Sus donc, mes Vers, chantez chants doloreux" (Rise up my Verses, sing painful songs, l. 50) that constitute a kind of refrain in the lament. Other important conventions are the convocation at the tomb, the flower offerings, and the evocation of nightfall at the end. Proper names in the poem such as Colin, Thenot, and Pan also come from the pastoral tradition as do plants, animals, and foods such as lilies, roses, swans, nightingales, crows, curdled milk, cheese. Marot on occasion blends Greek and Rhétoriqueur influences. For example, the catalog of cities that mourn Louise harks back to Moschus, but the alliteration, such as "Amboise en boit," recalls the Rhétoriqueurs. One also finds an example of the classical topic of the world turned upside-down in mourning, but that is probably inspired by Lemaire's "Plainte du désiré."

Despite such Rhétoriqueur traces, the poem is a full-scale reproduction of neoclassical pastoral conventions that stands in sharp contrast to the deploration. A good indication of Marot's profound understanding of Virgil's shift from mourning to panegyric is the new topic he creates. As E.Z. Lambert observes, "It is Marot who first brings together the traditional funereal convocation about the grave with the equally traditional pastoral inventory of sweets. In transferring the conventional recital of pastoral pleasures ('here are oaks and galingale, here sweetly hum the bees') to a specific locale within this landscape, the gravesite, the elegist says in the most emphatic possible way: here too are sweet things—or, perhaps rather, here too sweet things can be *brought*."[10] This poem with its sweet pastoral consolation could not be further from the grieving mourners of the deploration and the other complaints.

The style is also completely different. The pastoral is theoretically a low-style genre, but almost from the beginning, poets have played with its conventions to write elevated poetry. Whereas the low- and middle-style ornamentation creates a heteroclite medieval style in "The Deploration for Florimond Robertet," in the eclogue we have a consistent use of pastoral low-style conventions applied to lofty subject matter, the death of a queen. Take, for example, the lines that praise the queen mother as a peacemaker—traditionally a subject belonging to the high style:

> Tant bien y sut aux Lis joindre les Roses,
> Tant bien y sut bonnes Herbes semer,
> Tant bien savait confirmer
> Tout le Bétail de toute la Contrée,
> Tant bien savait son Parc clore & fermer
> Qu'on n'a point vu les Loups y faire entrée.
> (ll. 143–48)

(So well did she know how to join Lilies to Roses, / So well did she know how to sow good seed, / So well did she know how to strengthen / All of the Animals of the whole Country, / So well did she know how to enclose and lock her Park / That one did not see the Wolves enter therein.)

This poem, therefore, is the first of a French tradition of courtly pastoral: the peace of distant Arcadia now becomes the stability of the homeland under the monarch's protection.[11] Such, we should recall, was understood in the Middle Ages to be the message of Virgil's First Eclogue, which Marot translated and placed at the beginning of the *Adolescence*. The praises of Daphnis in Virgil's Fifth Eclogue may also have had political implications as an allusion to the apotheosis of the recently assassinated Julius Caesar.[12] Here even more clearly than in the translation of the First Eclogue Marot applies Virgilian pastoral themes of Roman imperial propaganda to the French monarchy in order to suggest a renewal of empire.

Nevertheless, despite the poem's solid Virgilian pedigree, Marot's shift to an easy consolation may have ironic overtones. It resembles the epitaph that begins "Celle qui travailla pour le repos de maint / Repose maintenant, pourquoi criez, Humains?" (She who worked for the rest of many / Now rests, why do you cry out, Humans?) (*O.D.*, CIV, ll. 1–2). Most critics see here an allusion to Louise's peacemaking role in the Treaty of Cambrai. P. Leblanc finds Marot's unquestioning acceptance of the necessity of death.[13] Only G. Guiffrey sees the possible irony in these lines.[14] Was Marot thinking of the avid queen mother's victims such as Semblançay?

Marot's praises of the education Louise gave to the daughters of the nobility may also contain touches of irony. Take, for example, the following lines:

> Oisiveté n'allez point nourrisant,
> Car elle est pire entre jeunes Bergères
> Qu'entre Brebis ce grand Loup ravissant
> Qui vient au soir toujours en ces Fougères!
> (ll. 77–80)

(Do not encourage indolence, / For it is worse among young shepherd-
esses / Than is among the sheep the great ravening wolf / That always
comes at evening to these thickets.)

Here Christian morality stands pastoral *otium* on its head.[15] There
is also perhaps a smiling reference to the hours of grueling toil that
the queen mother put her charges through.[16] Such possible ironies
save this poem from flatness. Otherwise it would ring hollow, especially in the *Suite,* where Robertet's disconsolate mourners remain
fresh in the reader's memory.

## Marot's Other Eclogues

It is convenient to leave temporarily the 1538 edition in order
briefly to consider Marot's other eclogues. The most important that
he wrote are the "Eclogue to the King under the Names Pan and
Robin" (*O.L.,* LXXXIX) and the eclogue written for the birth of
the Dauphin (*O.L.,* XC). In both poems, Marot emphasizes his role
as poet much in the tradition of Virgil's First Eclogue. The two
poems, however, show two very different uses of convention. The
former, written while Marot was basking in the sun of royal favor,
is a request to Francis I for a permanent lodging. There Marot
combines medieval and classical pastoral elements to imply complicity yet distance between himself and the monarch. Marot casts
himself as Robin, a figure from the medieval pastoral tradition,
whereas he casts Francis I as the classical god, Pan. His application
of pastoral conventions to both implies that both belong to the same
courtly pastoral world. His consistent distinction between medieval
pastoral for himself and classical pastoral for the monarch marks
their hierarchical distances within that world. This poem is famous
for its touching evocations of Marot's childhood and his idyllic
relationship with his father, yet it is not a Renaissance version of
Wordsworth's "Ode to Immortality." Here Marot looks forward to
the possibility of an even greater old age because his poetic talents
will come to full fruition with the king's support.[17]

When he wrote the eclogue for the dauphin, Marot was in exile
and perhaps already aware that he was about to die. He was also
writing for a very different audience—the future Henri II and his
Medici princess, Catherine, who were to support the Pléiade's neo-
classicism. Whereas the eclogue to the king artfully combined medieval and classical elements, now Marot writes a poem that is so

entirely in the French neoclassical elevated style that du Bellay considered it one of the best poems Marot had ever written. Some modern readers of Marot, however, find this poem as stiff-necked as the eclogue for Louise de Savoie, but the poem has real merits. An artful combination of elevation and pastoral lowness in the tradition of Virgil's Fourth Eclogue, it predicts that the new dauphin Francis—the future Francis II—will bring in a golden age. Despite—no, because of—the Virgilian overlay, such lines as the following have a haunting poignancy:

> O si tant vivre en ce monde je pusse
> Qu'avant mourir loisir de chanter j'eusse
> Tes nobles faits, ni Orpheus de Thrace,
> Ni Apollo, qui Orpheus efface,
> Ne me vaincrait, non pas Clio la belle,
> Ni le dieu Pan & Syringue, y fust elle.
>
> (ll. 89–93)

(O that I could live long enough in this world / That before dying, I had the leisure to sing / Your noble deeds, neither Orpheus of Thrace, / Nor Apollo, who wipes out Orpheus, / Would conquer me, nor the beautiful Clio, / Nor the god Pan and Syringue, were she there.)

Here Marot re-creates the full Renaissance tradition of the poet as *vates*. His poetic gift divines the dauphin's future great deeds because—in the Renaissance—they hold forth the possibility of epic poetry—the genre in which every Renaissance poet hoped to achieve artistic fulfillment. Thus the neoclassical sublimity of the poem is a burst of glory that transcends the poet's humble, pastoral place and cries out for patronage in a style worthy of the royal grandeur that augurs. Yet Marot has not assumed the posture of a solitary and alienated poet. Although the august and ancient poetic calling inhabits him, his destiny is not to go into isolation to write and sing, but rather to stand in the court company and to behold royal splendor.

## Chapter Seven
# Marot's Elegies

Marot's collection of twenty-one elegies in the 1533 *Suite* marks the serious beginning of the genre in French. The 1538 edition includes six more poems. The word *elegy* in Greek originally referred to a prosodic form: a hexameter followed by a pentameter, but it subsequently referred to such a wide variety of poems that a definition is virtually impossible. With the advent of vernacular poetry, even the verse form disappeared. Marot originally used the word to refer to a long, sad, erotic love poem. Three of the elegies he added in 1538 enlarged the genre to include death. Although some scholars have referred to joyous elegies, we have been unable to find any. Even the happiest elegies in Marot's collection are tinted with doubt, frustration, or dissatisfaction. It makes sense that these poems follow the two funeral poems in the *Suite* for at least two reasons. First of all, they are lower in subject matter. Second, like the complaints, the elegies deal with the frustrations of love and death. The elegies dealing uniquely with love are verse epistles. Those dealing with death are narrative fables.[1]

The love elegies' level of style is Marot's version of what Ronsard will later call his *beau style bas*.[2] J.P. Houston identifies this as the *genus subtile floridius* (the somewhat ornamented low style).[3] The adjective *floridus*, it should be recalled, originally applied to the middle style, and in many ways, it would seem more appropriate to call these flowery poems middle style. Yet there is a long tradition that assigns love poetry to the low style, and Marot in the guise of the knight of Pavia refers to the style as "piteux" (wretched or miserable, *O.L.*, LII, l. 106) as opposed to the high style of victorious war poetry. We shall also see that the lowness of the genre is one of the main characteristics that distinguish the death elegy from the more elevated complaints.

## The Elegies in the Form of Love Epistles

Sebillet is probably thinking of these poems when he compares the elegy to the epistle. For there are frequent allusions to writing

82

and letters throughout Marot's collection. Contradictions in Sebillet's definition of the elegy seem to allude to its ornamented yet low style that is both simple and formal. In contrast to an epistle about love that is not an elegy, the elegy expresses emotions directly (*nuement*), simply (*simplement*), and does not have what Sebillet calls "subscriptions" and "superscriptions." Yet it is in a less "popular" style than the epistle.[4] We shall return to Sebillet's distinction between elegy and epistle in the following chapter.

Despite their classical name, the elegies have been called the most medieval part of Marot's work. Indeed, they are a far cry from the frank sensuality of the Roman elegy. They draw on the full panoply of techniques and conventions that R. Dragonetti finds in the *trouvère* love song. The woman is on a pedestal. She is the remote "Lady" whose great beauty may seem beyond the lover's reach. Cupid himself falls in love with her. In one poem, she is the most beautiful woman in the world. She may be cruel, ungrateful, or welcoming. She has the power to grant "merci." The lover is constant and long-suffering. The lover and lady are constantly under the threat of false lovers and slanderers out to smear the lady's reputation. The lover and the lady exchange hearts. The god of love is Cupid, blindfolded and with bow and arrow.

The vocabulary of love in the elegies draws on many of the same domains as that of the *trouvères:* war, the hunt, the feudal relationship between lord and lady (the lover "serves" the lady), medicine (love is a wound that needs a cure), and religion (the lovers meet on Christmas eve, love is a martyrdom). Love, a kind of dying, is opposed to reason. It is compared and contrasted to fire, ice, and light—*trouvère* as well as Petrarchan motifs. Marot also draws on various *trouvère* topoi. The *trouvères* contrasted their love to the month of May. At the departure of his lady, Marot finds that even the month of May is sad. The poet also indulges in a medieval as opposed to classical pastoral fantasy: the knight making love to a peasant girl. Finally, the very epistolary nature of these poems harks back to the *trouvères.* The envois of the older poems already mark them as letters to be sent to the beloved.[5]

However, it can be difficult to separate medieval from classical conventions in the collection. Marot's vision of nature belongs to the tradition of the *locus amoenus*—a classical topos that was a *trouvère* favorite—the pleasant place where love can grow. To express the constancy or intensity of his love, he evokes another *trouvère* favorite inherited from the classics, the topic of *adynata* (impossible happenings in nature, such as the rivers reversing their courses). Many of the stylistic procedures of the elegies also recall medieval as well as classical love poetry: Marot's *sententia*, antitheses, hyperbole, and comparisons to great models of history, myth, and legend such as Dido, Medea, and Sappho. Certain obstacles of love—the lady is married, the lovers are forced to separate, the lady loves another— also exist in Ovid and Propertius as well as the *trouvères* and troubadours. Thus it is possible that the *trouvères* and troubadours also imitate classical authors in the indirect creative way that Marot does. By the Renaissance, creative license to imitate the ancients may have been taken so much for granted by poets that readers did not notice what we call medieval conventions in these usages any more than medieval spectators detected anachronism in the medieval costumes that clothe biblical characters in Gothic art.

**Marot and Ovid.** Twentieth-century readers, on the other hand, are blinded by medieval conventions. J. E. Clark goes so far as to characterize Marot's use of elegy as a "disguise" for conventional love epistles.[6] As in the other genres, Marot's imitations are much more indirect than those of later poets such as Ronsard. Specific allusions to Roman elegy—as well as, by the way, Petrarch—are at best scattered and unimportant. Sebillet, however, must have a different kind of imitation in mind when he writes that Marot's epistle-elegies are so much an image of Ovid's *Amores* that only the words distinguish them.[7] Modern scholars in general disagree with this perception. C. Scollen considers Ovid's *Heroides* to be Marot's true model.[8] Yet Sebillet seems to make a distinction between the *Heroides* and the elegies when he says that "Ovid's epistles (the *Heroides*) are true, sad epistles about love but cannot be called elegies."[9] If there is a copy of a *Heroide* in Marot's elegies, it is Maguelonne's epistle.

Although we may find the resemblance unconvincing, we must always be ready to acknowledge that Marot copies Ovid in a way we would not expect. For example, the collection's first elegy, which a knight wounded and taken prisoner at the Battle of Pavia addresses his mistress (*O.L.*, LII), bears some striking similarities to the first elegy in Ovid's *Amores*. Ovid tells us how he set out to write about war in hexameters, but could not because Cupid kept kicking off the last foot of the second verse of each couplet, obliging him to write about love. The knight at Pavia too says he must now sing of love because the defeat at Pavia has left him nothing military to sing of, but he will return to war if the occasion arises:

> Lors conviendra dancer d'un autre branle,
> Laisser faudra Bois, Sources et Ruisseaux,
> Laisser faudra Chasse, Chiens & Oiseaux,
> Laisser faudra d'Amours les petits dons
> Pour suivre aux Champs Etendards & Guidons.
>
> (ll. 128–32)

(Then it will be time to dance to another tune, / To leave Woods, Fountains, and Brooks, / To leave Hunting, Dogs & Birds / To leave Love's little gifts / To follow in the Fields Standards and Banners.)

Although the expression is very different, the theme is the same. The poet of the elegy is a frustrated epic poet who must settle for less. It is all the more complicated to see here because Marot adds a new dimension. The knight of Pavia not only sings of war and love, he also makes both. Thus there is a subtle slippage between writing and deeds. In the above lines, it is unclear whether the knight means that he will change the subject of his songs or of his actions. Because both poems come at the beginning of their collections, however, they identify the elegy as a love poem of a lesser genre than poetry dealing with war.

Scholars have tended to overlook such allusions to convention in their quest to reconstruct Marot's biography. For a long time it was thought that Marot himself had been taken prisoner, but we now realize that, as a poet, he was not a good candidate for ransom. Another theory holds that Marot wrote the poem in someone else's name. Whether or not such is the case, we consider the character of the knight who gives up fighting for writing as an attempt to update the Ovidian elegiac convention.

Scholarly attempts—now generally discredited—to determine the identity of the ladies to whom the elegies are written have also obscured Marot's different manners of treating love. Rather than grouping poems according to some fictitious lady, we find it more fruitful to determine how love is treated differently according to genre. We have already considered the differences between the rondeaux and the songs. The elegy in its ornamented low style offers us still another approach. The following elegy is written because

the lover no longer receives any news from the lady—the situation
we have already seen in a rondeau and a song (see pp. 60–61 and
pp. 66–67) and shall also see in a verse-epistle that is not an elegy.
Here, however, Marot does not defuse his feelings with wit and
intellectual considerations as he does in the rondeaux. Nor does he
write a cry from the heart with little ornamentation. Rather he
combines an evocation of intense feeling with a formal style.

> Qu'ai-je méfait, dites, ma chère Amie?
> Votre Amour semble être tout endormie.
> Je n'ai de vous plus lettres ni langage;
> Je n'ai de vous un seul petit message;
> Plus ne vous vois aux lieux accoutumés.
> Sont ja éteints vos désirs allumés,
> Qui avec moi d'un même feu ardaient?
> Où sont ces yeux lesquels me regardaient,
> Souvent en ris, souvent avec larmes?
> Où sont les mots qui tant m'ont fait d'alarmes?
> Où est la bouche aussi qui m'appaisait?
> Quand tant de fois & si bien me baisait?
> Où est le coeur que [sic] irrévocablement
> M'avait donné? Où est semblablement
> La blanche main qui bien fort m'arrêtait
> Quand de partir de vous besoin m'était?
> Hélas (Amants) hélas, se peut-il faire
> Qu'Amour si grand se puisse ainsi défaire?
> Je penserais plutôt que les Ruisseaux
> Feraient aller encontre mont leurs eaux,
> Considérant que de fait ni pensée
> Ne l'ai encor' (que je sache) offensée.
> Doncques [sic], Amour, qui couves sous tes ailes
> Journellement les coeurs des Demoiselles,
> Ne laisse pas trop refroidir celui
> De celle la pour qui j'ai tant d'ennui.
> Ou trompe-moi, en me faisant entendre
> Qu'elle a le coeur bien ferme, et fût-il tendre.
>                                    (O.L., LVIII)

(What did I do wrong, tell me, my dear Friend? / Your love seems to
be completely asleep. / I have from you neither letters nor language; / I
have from you not a single little message; / No longer do I see you in the
usual places. / Is the desire kindled in your heart now extinguished / That

with me of a common fire burned? / Where are these eyes that used to look at me, / Often laughing, often with tears?/ Where are the words that so often alarmed me? / Where is the mouth that so often soothed me? / When so many times and so well you kissed me? / Where is the heart that irrevocably / You gave me that so strongly stopped me / When I had to leave you? / Helas (Lovers) helas, can it be / That Love so great can thus come undone? / I thought that sooner would Brooks / Make their waters run upstream, / Considering that in neither deed nor thought / Have I yet (as far as I know) offended her. / Therefore, Love, who gathers under your wings / Everyday the hearts of Demoiselles, / Do not let cool down the one / Of her for whom I suffer such anguish. / Or trick me, in making me understand / That she has a firm heart, even though it were tender.)

This poem belongs to the first of the cycles—that of the Forgetful One (Elegies I–VIII)—that V.L. Saulnier finds in the elegies. The others are those of the Rebel (Elegies IX–XIII), the Woman with Ulterior Motives (Elegy XIV), the Too Well Guarded One (Elegies XV–XVII), and the Misguided One (Elegies XVIII–XXbis).[10] Many scholars have criticized Saulnier's attempt, but it still represents the best analysis of the collection's structure to date. Furthermore, it is based on the correct observation that Marot's collection suggests works such as Martial d'Auvergne's *Arrêts d'Amour,* the Rhétoriqueurs' *Doctrinaux,* and the debates that work out a "casuistry" of love.[11]

The meandering thoughts of this casuistry constitute a discourse that is more passionate than that of the witty rondeau built on various greetings, but more fully argued than the song we have considered. The poem is the shortest of the elegies, except for Elegy X in the 1538 edition, which is in the form of a ballade.[12] This ballade however, is more of a prelude to Elegy XI than a separate poem in itself. Yet its rhymed couplets give rise to an ornamented development of amorous casuistry that Marot avoids in the more suggestive songs, such as the one we have analyzed on the same theme. The rhymed couplets, by the way, are not a necessary condition for the development of amorous casuistry. Compare, for example, the strophic elegy, Elegy XIX (*O.L.,* LXIX), which passionately works out themes in the manner of the rhymed-couplet elegies, and the lighter songs which make a freer, more suggestive use of strophic form.

The poem works out in fuller form Fabri's schema for the "lettre d'amour vicieuse" that Marot only suggests in the song. It is also more anguished. The poet praises the lady for her beauty and the quality of her love. He praises himself by protesting his constancy and innocence, but instead of requesting that she not be angry, he prays that she not stop loving him—the fear he repressed in the song. The poem develops these themes in the usual epistolary structure of a prologue, a narration, and a petition. It also draws on another of Fabri's explanations according to which the letter is divided into three parts: the cause (a person's reason for writing), the intention (a person's wishes), and the conclusion. The cause corresponds to the prologue and narration, the intention to the petition.[13] The poet's cause for writing is that he no longer hears from the lady. His intention is to protest his innocence; the conclusion is that she should not stop loving him. In this case, the cause and the intention correspond to the narration; the conclusion, to the petition.

   **Ornament.**   The way in which Marot expands into this epistolary structure is a good example of a method of amplification (characteristic of medieval poetry) called ornamental variation: repeating the same idea in various rhetorical modes.[14] The prologue (only the first two lines) announces the themes of the intention (the poet's innocence) and the petition (the lady's loss of love). The narration (ll. 3–22) repeats both of these themes as well as that of the lady's physical and verbal absence. However, instead of stating in one line that he no longer hears from the lady, Marot amplifies by what the rhetoricians would call division. He "divides" the experience into its various parts. Compare lines 3–16 with line 2 from the song ("No longer do you write, no longer do you ask about me"). Now the poet has neither letters, words, a message, nor the physical presence of the lady: her eyes, laugh, words, mouth, heart, or hand. This enumeration of the different parts of the lady is of course an example of a blason in which one describes the body from head to foot. At the same time, it works in praises of the lady.

   The theme of the lady's loss of love that appears in lines 6–7, lines 17–20, and lines 23–28—but with different rhetorical ornament—is an example of a phenomenon in Marot's elegies that one could call a thematic refrain.[15] Marot makes a particularly artistic use of interrogation to mark a varying tonality. In lines 6–7, we have the interrogation as well as the contrasts between kindling and extinguishing fire. In lines 17–20, the theme is really used to lead up to the main subject of the verse paragraph, the poet's innocence. Here too is an interrogation, but now it is in sententious form as opposed to the more direct question of lines 6–7. It goes beyond the specific case to communicate a kind of cosmic anguish that the loss of such a love inspires. The interjective apostrophe to lovers and the classical world-upside-down topos of brooks reversing their flow also gives this impression. In both cases, the interrogations communicate disbelief. Marot gives this disbelief a curious twist in the petition (ll. 23–28). Instead of asking whether the lady's love has gone out, the poet prays to the God of love that he either not let her love die or at least make the poet think that it has not. This irony is typical of the elegies, and opens up the poem to many interpretations. Is the poet so sure that the lady no longer loves him that he wants to hide his head in the sand? Is the prayer to be deceived actually an acknowledgment that the poet cannot love the lady enough to trust her, or does it simply imply that he loves her so much that he does not even want to consider the possibility she has cooled? It is better not to try to pin the poet down. His brooding tone here, however, is to be contrasted with the delicate refusal to consider such a possibility in the song or the witty mask that hides the poet's worry in the rondeau.

**Lowness.** Although this elegy does not use a full range of devices inherited from formal medieval love poetry, its relatively simple, almost conversational syntax gives it a lowness absent from Marot's more ceremonious predecessors. Neither images, allegory, obscure erudition, nor rhetorical procedures encumber forward conversational movement. The repeated interrogations, for example, give the poem an almost childlike quality. Unlike the sublime *trouvère* poems, it creates the impression of a more human relation with the lady. Although she is on a pedestal, she is not entirely out of reach. Here, therefore, we have an ornamented low style that brings down the formal strain of medieval love poetry in contrast to the songs that raise a popular form to a level of courtly refinement. We shall consider how the popular low style of the epistles differs from that of the songs as well as from the ornamented low style of the elegies in the following chapter.

## The Death Elegies

The death elegies expand the Renaissance concept of the genre as love poetry to include the classical subject of death. According to Sebillet, the death elegy is a complaint in the form of an elegy just as the eclogue from Louise de Savoie is a complaint in the form of an eclogue. Thus we believe that the C.A. Mayer edition oversimplifies matters in its classification of the death elegies as complaints instead of elegies. They are both. They are like the other complaints because they show us disconsolate mourners: they are different in that they feature a narrative of how the departed died and are written in a lower style.

**Fables about dying.** In terms of the manner of death, the 1538 order of the poems follows the descending progression of the elements: quintessence, fire, air, water, and earth. Anne L'Huilier of the first elegy dies in a fire and her soul goes to the quintessential heaven. Semblançay of the second dies hanging in the air. Jean Chauvin of the third is drowned in the water and buried in the earth. Furthermore, all three poems are narratives with morals either at the beginning or at the end. The narratives follow the rhetorical model of the pragmatographia, which dictates that in describing an event one should describe the time before the event, the time of the event itself, and the consequences of the event.[16] In each case the central event is the death of the victim. Descriptions of the time before death deal with causes and reasons. The evocation of the time after death deals with the reactions of the mourners. The elegy for Semblançay gives a curious twist to the subject. Since it is the hanging man himself who speaks, he takes the place of the disconsolate mourner. He describes his body as it decays on the gallows— a distinct reference to the "Epitaphe Villon" better known as the "Ballade des Pendus"—and he issues a moralistic but bitter call to prayer.

**Ornamented lowness.** The death elegies like the other complaints recall more formal poems. Especially striking is the Rhétoriqueur-inspired wit and wordplay in the early poems. For example, Anne L'Huilier's and Semblançay's names are appropriate to their deaths in fire and in Fortune's realm of false semblances, respectively, but Marot does nothing to develop the obvious. The mythology in these poems—Venus, Mars, and the water deities of the Seine—also bears the stamp of the Rhétoriqueurs. In the elegy for Semblançay, the images of Fortune as a nursing mother and hangwoman come from Lady Reason's speech in the *Romance of the Rose.*[17] Although the elegy for Jean Chauvin, on the other hand, is in a more neutral style characteristic of Marot's later poetry, it harks back to the Misenus episode from Virgil's *Aeneid,* 6.162–74. Despite such ornament, however, the poems are of a distinctly lower style than the other complaints because Marot's rapid, even unseemly humorous *badinage* evokes the kind of tension between lament and consolation, feelings and doctrine we have already seen. This *badinage,* however, communicates not so much the cavalier attitude toward death that C. Martineau-Génieys has suggested, as a laughter among tears of tenderness for the victims, reminiscent of the plain-style epitaphs. In the elegy for Anne L'Huilier, Marot communicates a smiling yet melancholy tenderness for both Anne and her husband—smiling through the gallant Petrarchan conceits playing on fire and water, melancholy in the image of the tears the husband sheds even though his wife's soul is in heaven. Marot's wit, more subtle in the elegy for Semblançay, plays against Reason's moralizing about Fortune, which is inspired by the more formal *Romance of the Rose.* The question of whether the victim was justly or unjustly treated is never resolved because it is Semblançay himself, not the poet, who speaks. We cannot tell whether he is a self-indulgent criminal like Villon's "pendus" or an innocent victim fortifying his soul with Reason's warnings about Fortune.

The low-style elements in the elegy for Jean Chauvin are the graceful ease of the narrative and the reason for the victim's death. The river nymphs of the Seine fall in love with him and their husbands overturn his boat out of a jealousy reminiscent of humorous fabliau-type satires on women. This graceful, smiling lowness, however, does not imply a serene acceptance of death as C. Martineau-Génieys has suggested.[18] After the victim is drowned, the water nymphs who loved him wash his body with tears and return him to earth. There his friends thank God for having taken him out of this woeful terrestrial existence—the least comforting of all consolations, according to death in "The Deploration for Florimond Robertet" (*O.L.,* VI, ll. 449–52). The poem's easy, charming grace, therefore, communicates a smiling, melancholy tenderness about the departed. It suggests that death is a complicated tragedy that causes the living both to laugh and to cry, to hope and to mourn.

Marot's death elegies manifest the same sort of tensions between lament and consolation as the other complaints, but they are elegies because this tension is so adroitly based on his artful juxtaposition of high- and low-style elements. Unlike the other complaints, however, which are poems in a high-style genre that Marot simplifies and humanizes, the death elegies are definitely low-style poems in which low-style elements almost jarringly undermine the seriousness of formal elements in the narratives.

## Chapter Eight

# The Epistles and the End of the *Suite*

## The Epistles of the *Suite*

In the epistles of the *Suite,* Marot is freer with convention and protocol than in the corresponding section of the *Adolescence.* He conveys an impression of ease and nonchalance that is reflected in the arrangement and tone of the poems. In contrast to the formal hierarchies of the *Adolescence,* the epistles of the *Suite* fall into vague undefinable cycles. Furthermore, as opposed to the sometimes belabored epistles of the earlier section, those of the *Suite* all portray Marot as a consummate master of both poetry and court politics. The reader has the impression that the struggling poet of the *Adolescence* has now arrived at the pinnacle of success.

The epistles of the *Suite* contain a large variety of styles and voices. In the epistles for the "affaire des dames," Marot argues for a level of wit and satire that does not descend to name-calling and insult. As we have seen in the epistle for Lyon Jamet, his plain or low style is not a crass style. Some of the epistles hark back to more conventional forms such as the ceremonial praises for Eleanor or the witty Rhétoriqueur play on words for the Chancellor Du Prat—the man's name also means "prairie." Other epistles include petitions for Marot's friends, such as the epistle to Montmorency where Marot asks for a job for the late Queen Claude's tailor. Others are circumstantial banter, such as the poem that Marot writes because he lost at playing cards. In many, Marot writes deftly, adapting the voices of others: Pierre Vuyart who asks Madame Lorraine for a horse, or the little princess of Navarre writing to her mother.

The three epistles to the king are the most famous poems in the collection and deserve special attention. We shall also consider the epistle to two maidens, an example of Sebillet's popular-style love poetry.

**Love in the plain style.**   The epistle written to two maidens
(*Epîtres,* XLIX) seems to correspond to Sebillet's definition of a love
epistle that is not an elegy. It has a subscription (ll. 1–4) and asks
the two maidens to write. This is the same request we have considered in the rondeaux, chansons, and elegies. The style is not
popular in the same sense as the songs. We believe that Sebillet
uses the word *popular* to refer to the witty distance from feeling that
is characteristic of the plain style and that we have already seen in
the *Adolescence* epistles and in the rondeaux. Marot writes to two
women, not one, and adopts a simple, almost childlike tone with
a very short verse line. Here is an example:

> Ecrivez-moi
> Donc, je vous prie;
> Car l'Enfant crie,
> Quand on lui faut.
> (ll. 16–19)

(Write to me / Then, please; / Because a Child cries / When someone
disappoints him.)

**Epistles to the king: complicity and distance.**   The epistles
Marot wrote during his second imprisonment and after having been
robbed are considered masterpieces of conversational wit, in which
the plain style techniques that were so successful in the epistle to
Lyon Jamet are now sharpened and refined. In these, Marot's confidence in royal protection—which we have already seen in the arrogant epistle to Bouchard—translates into casual, witty chats with
the king. Here too he expects to obtain satisfaction on the basis of
who he is rather than what he has done. As in the epistle to Bouchard, Marot's arrogant silence implies belief in a distance between
him, a man of the court, and the representatives of canon and secular
law. Now, however, his witty chats suggest confidence in a complicity, but not equality, between him and the king as two men
above the law. This delicate balance of complicity and distance is
a hallmark of the plain style. Marot carries it to a fine art, not only
in the epistles, but also, as we shall see, in the epigrams. On the
other hand, the epistle Marot wrote to succeed his father is of a
more serious nature and lacks the confidence in his audience necessary to the plain style. It is nevertheless a very moving poem.

The first of these epistles to appear in the *Suite* is the one Marot wrote when he was imprisoned for helping a prisoner to escape from the watch (*Epîtres,* XI).

The prologue of this epistle begins with a brief, casual salutation and immediately sets a tone of intimate familiarity through a judicious use of asides and punning wordplay:

> Roi des Français, plein de toutes bontés,
> Quinze jours a (je les ai bien comptés),
> Et dès demain seront justement seize,
> Que je fus fait Confrère au Diocèse
> De saint Marry, en l'Eglise saint Pris.
>
> (ll. 1–5)

(King of the French, full of all goodness, / Fifteen days ago (I have counted everyone of them), / Tomorrow it will be exactly sixteen, / I was made a brother in the diocese / Of Saint Grieved, in the Church of Saint Captured.)

The narration traces events from Marot's imprisonment to his present situation. Marot was arrested for having helped a prisoner escape from the watch. Thus he owed two debts to society—a payment to the guards for the inconvenience and a debt to the king for having broken the law. Lines 8–42 lead up to Marot's debt to the king. Despite his sparkling wit, Marot's argument is clear and hard-nosed—he has paid the guards so he just needs a word from the king to go free. Thus he is really writing about a very minor matter of justice for a person of his importance and refuses to go into the details of a defense. (Here, as in the epistle to Bouchard, Marot considers that his relationship to the court puts him above the law.) He says he denied any wrongdoing to those who came to arrest him because had he acknowledged it, they would have "heard" him. (They would have remembered his every word.) Besides, he says, how could he help deliver a prisoner when he could not free himself (ll. 20–26)? When he broaches the subject of his debt to the king, he simply puts all arguments aside—"I believe you if I did wrong" (l. 51)—and points out that his offense is worthy only of a fine.

The passage is famous for its rich variety of tone and rapid art of description and storytelling, both characteristics of the plain style.

Most often noted are Marot's feigned naïveté, mock ignorance, and surprise. Marot keeps up the pace with a variety of techniques— parenthetical asides or narrative infinitives (l. 20)—that prefigure the best of La Fontaine. He is also a master of the significant gesture:

> Sur mes deux bras ils ont la main posée,
> Et m'ont mené ainsi que [sic] une Epousée;
> Non pas ainsi, mais plus raide un petit.
>                                        (ll. 29–31)

(On my two arms they placed their hands / And led me off like a Bride; / Well, not exactly, but a little more roughly.)

The rhymes in general, while avoiding Rhétoriqueur mechanics, remain extraordinarily rich.

The petition is brief as is the prologue. Marot asks first for a letter to free him and then makes what begins as a very formal apology, although it turns to fun: "I did not go to speak to you / Because I did not have the time to go" (ll. 67–68).

The epistle that Marot wrote to Francis I on having been robbed (*Epîtres*, XXV) is another example of wit used to imply a delicate balance of complicity and distance. Instead of appealing above the law, however, Marot now appeals to the monarch above the head of Fortune herself—a perspective that allows him the necessary distance for his sparkling humor. As in the previously considered epistle, the prologue is rapid and to the point. After uttering the maxim that ill fortune comes in twos and threes, Marot recalls the king's own bad fortune, implying that they have something in common. Yet at the same time he makes sure to mark the hierarchical differences between them.

The narration (ll. 8–78) is a model of rapid wit, gesture, and portrait. Marot begins with a masterful portrait of the valet who robbed him. An artful enumeration first of the valet's vices and then of his so-called virtues, it owes its effectiveness to Marot's delicate ear for rhyme, rhythm, and alliteration:

> J'avais un jour un Valet de Gascogne,
> Gourmand, Ivrogne, & assuré Menteur,

> Pipeur, Larron, Jureur, Blasphémateur,
> Sentant la Hart de cent pas à la ronde.
>
> (ll. 8–11)

(I had one day a Valet from Gascony, / Gourmand, Drunkard, and for sure a Liar, / Trickster, Thief, Swearer, Blasphemer, / Smelling the hangman's noose at a hundred paces.)

Marot's description of the theft itself is distinguished by its colorful language. He calls the valet by the dialectical term "Hillot" (l. 15) and says that his purse full of money was a "tumor" that the valet stuck under an armpit. There is also Marot's statement of the obvious—the valet, he says, took the purse, not intending to give it back "because I have not heard anything about it since" (ll. 22–23).

The description of the clothes the valet took is another example of Marot's masterful plain-style art of understatement and parenthetical asides. After enumerating all the clothes, he says in lines 27–30:

> De mes Habits (en effet) il pilla
> Tous les plus beaux, & puis s'en habilla
> Si justement, qu'à le voir ainsi être,
> Vous l'eussiez pris (en plein jour) pour son Maître.

(Of my clothes (in fact) he pillaged / All the best looking, and then put them on / So well, that to see him thus / You would have taken him (in broad daylight) for his Master.)

After mentioning that the valet took the best of his horses, he sums up once again by stating the obvious. The valet, he says, forgot nothing except to say good-bye (l. 36).

In the narration of his illness (ll. 49–78), Marot communicates the overwhelming nature of his misfortune through an adroit use of polyptoton ("assaillir, assaut, saut") and punning: the illness, he says, almost sent him "Rimer sous terre & y faire des Vers" (To rhyme in the underworld and make Verses / Worms there, l. 53). Also remarkable is his description of his sick body (ll. 60–61) and the doctors' diagnosis. If he does not get well by spring, they tell him, he will die in winter. He sums up at the beginning of the petition with the pun "That's how I have been treated over the last nine months" (ll. 79–80).

The petition (ll. 79–129) is another masterpiece of irony. Marot asks not a gift, but a "loan" that he will pay back when everyone is happy or when the king will no longer be famous, and then he finishes with a mock formal celebration of the king.

We have space to consider only very briefly the epistle Marot wrote to Francis I to succeed his father (*Epîtres*, XII). The two we have just considered cause critics unjustly to denigrate Marot's timidity here.[1] Only J. Plattard and R. Griffin have seen that despite his melancholy, Marot does maintain a certain humorous distance.[2] The negative judgments are insensitive to Marot's extremely delicate situation. The king had ordered that he replace his late father, Jean, on the rolls of the royal household, but the order had not been carried out. Marot, therefore, could no longer be confident of the whimsical monarch's support, which had kept him above the vicissitudes of life. The plain style mask, which assumes complicity between reader and writer, is therefore inappropriate. Here as in the last eclogue he wrote, Marot resorts to formality when in difficulty. And here too, he movingly recalls that his very sacred poetic calling—conferred upon him by his father—justifies his requests for support. Everyone who truly wishes to hear the poet's voice should read it.

**Marot's satirical epistles.**   This group consists of the four coqs-à-l'âne and Frippelippes's epistle to Sagon. Of these, only the first was published in the 1538 edition; but it is fitting to consider them together, and we are making an exception to our usual format. Marot's satirical poetry has been unfairly criticized for its lack of thematic originality and realist perspicacity in comparison to Rabelais or Coquillart.[3] To compare Marot to Rabelais, however, is to overlook the difference between lyric poetry and narrative discourse, the genre that holds a mirror to reality. As we have already seen, Marot maintains a distance from reality as is consistent with his conception of the poet's calling. In the poems under consideration, Marot's originality and richness come from the ways he creates that distance in a satirical context.

Although Marot called only the first coq-à-l'âne an epistle, C.A. Mayer has convincingly shown that all four poems belong to the epistolary genre.[4] The poet dates the poem, addresses it to a friend, pretends to fill him in on the latest news, asks how he is, and so

on. Such precisions, however, are entirely fictitious. Thus the coq-
à-l'âne is a parody of the epistle.

According to Thomas Sebillet's *Art Poétique*,[5] Marot invented this
genre, which seems calculated to create a protective distance between
author and reader. The name comes from the French proverb *sauter
du coq à l'âne* ("to skip from the cock to the ass") because of an
"inconstant variety of incoherent propositions." The content consists
of people's vices which are described vaguely and anonymously ("sont
repris librement par la suppression du nom de l'auteur"). The greater
the absurdity of its developments, the greater its elegance. It is to
be written in rhymed octosyllabic couplets.

Several of Marot's contemporaries took up his example—Eustorg
de Beaulieu, Lyon Jamet, La Salle, Claude Colet, and Pernette du
Guillet. But the Pléiade consigned the genre to oblivion for two
reasons. First of all, as may be seen in du Bellay's *Défense et illustration
de la langue française,* they protested Sebillet's application of the term
to the satires of Juvenal, Persius, and Horace. Sebillet says that
these poets wrote Latin coqs-à-l'âne. Second, they found it insig-
nificant and ineffective. For example, Peletier says that it embitters
rather than reforms those that it attacks.[6]

Marot's models come from the medieval dramatic genres of the
sottie and the fatrasie, favorites of the *basochiens* and *enfants sans
souci*.[7] The *sottie* in particular provides a precedent for devices of
protective distancing. It is fast moving, elliptical, and full of suggestive innuendos.[8] Jokes interrupt the forward development at times
when the satire is about to become too clear. The dialogue form of
the *sottie,* according to Plattard, seems another precedent for the
coq-à-l'âne, which can often be read as a conversation between two
people.[9]

The poems throw together a variety of topics in an incoherent
jumble. Marot takes on the doctrines and hypocritical practices of
Rome; the pretentions, bigotry, and ignorance of the Sorbonne; the
laziness and unchastity of the religious; and the absurd ambitions
of the military.

Scattered through such serious topics are reflections on women,
weather, love, and Marot's personal situation, as well as fleeting
references to usury, sloppy grammar at court, incompetent schoolmasters, and different well-known persons at the time. There are
also proverbs and first lines of popular songs. Many of the allusions—
especially in the fourth coq-à-l'âne—refer to people, events, and

situations long since forgotten. They are incomprehensible to us now. The third coq-à-l'âne is the clearest. It divides into large sections devoted to the theologian Noel Beda, Marot's rival Sagon, Marot's flight, and reflections on the rivalry between France and the Holy Roman Empire.

The coq-à-l'âne is an instance of the plain-style complicity between reader and addressee carried to such an extreme that it results in obscurity. In marked contrast to the epistle for Lyon Jamet, all four coq-à-l'âne poems, also addressed to Marot's good friend, are nearly incomprehensible. The artistic essence of the genre is to wrap all these reflections in an atmosphere of folly.[10] The poems group quite naturally into couplets and quatrains that Marot either juxtaposes with no connection or joins together with logical connectors ("so that," "however," "therefore," etc.) so as to suggest relationships that in fact do not exist. On the other hand, there are underlying relationships which it becomes a game to perceive beneath the apparent disarray. The poems progress at an extremely fast dramatic pace interspersed with ironic apostrophes, mock questions, proverbs, extravagant rhymes, paradoxes, and passing, confiding asides. The result reminds one of a chansonnier in a modern French nightclub who comes on the stage talking as fast as possible and alluding to the whole range of contemporary people, places, things, and events. A feigned naive irony pervades everywhere. As Vianey has noticed,[11] it gives du Bellay the example of praising what one wants to blame and counseling those whom one wants to criticize.

Yet it would be a mistake to make of Marot H. Guy's "courtier in the opposition."[12] Rather he writes from a position above events with an antiestablishment, aristocratic disdain characteristic of courts with real power. We have already seen Marot appeal above the heads of theologians and men of law to the king. His criticisms of the monastic orders fall within the range of the original meaning of reformation—a noble person's reform of a monastery or convent so that the inhabitants actually observe their vows of poverty, chastity, and obedience. Marot's denunciations of papists, papal greed, and hypocrisy also have a long tradition in the land of Pragmatic Sanction of Bourges. However, critics have been too hasty in interpreting mentions of the Antichrist, Babylon, and the she-ass of Jerusalem as allusions to the papacy. Marot does not make that association and could just as easily be referring to Luther.

The reflections on war and unruly soldiers do indeed mouth the attitudes of the common people who suffer from territorial ambitions as P. Vianey has said.[13] But they also recall Erasmus's ideas on defensive war and a desirable harmony of Christian princes—ideas, by the way, that permeate Rabelais's description of the Picrocholine war in *Gargantua*. As a poet Marot understood himself to be free to criticize. He even makes the distinction between religious progressivism and treason when he criticizes the Roman loyalists for confusing the two (second coq-à-l'âne, ll. 60–63). Yet as we have seen in the epistle to the king from Ferrara, such a discourse was no longer possible at the time because of the king's decision to persecute rather than to listen and tolerate.

Marot wrote "The Epistle of Frippelippes" (*O.S.*, VI) during a better time in 1537 after his return from exile. The historical context of the epistle has been discussed above (pp. 12–13 and pp. 17–18) and need not be repeated here. Marot pretends that it is his valet Frippelippes who answers Sagon since a reply to such a second-rate poet is hardly worthy of the master himself.

Frippelippes says that there are a host of people against his master. They do not include Saint-Gelais, Héroet, Rabelais, and Scève, however, but rather *un tas de jeunes Veaux* (a pile of young calves)— newcomers trying to establish themselves. He says that their works are so bad that their poor quality is their own best refutation.

Frippelippes then accuses Sagon of trying to destroy his master so as to get a better ecclesiastical post and decries Huet for trying to obtain Marot's position of valet de chambre. The resemblance of Sagon's name to "Sagouin" gives occasion for calling him a monkey. Sagon's work, says Frippelippes, deserves not corrections but a single line drawn through it from beginning to end. He says that Sagon has the eyes of a Frog and is the son of a Jew—Sagon had said that France was the only country free of Jews. He compares—unfavorably—Sagon to the valet who robbed Marot, accuses Sagon of having syphilis and of having stolen the title "coup d'essai." He says that even Sagon's chant royal that won the prize at the Puy de Rouen was written by his master, Marot.

Frippelippes then laughs at Sagon's naïveté in thinking that Marot would never come back to France, gives him a symbolic beating, challenges him to reply, and concludes. He says that Sagon has had a great enough honor in receiving an epistle from Marot's valet and trembles at the thought that his master will accuse him of beating a dead ass.

Critics consider this poem Marot's masterpiece in the satirical genre. It is his sole reply in the great controversy that swirled about him, but he brilliantly manages to keep his position above events in writing an artificial epistle. The fiction of the valet has many advantages. It puts Sagon in his place. (In fact, it threw him on an uneasy defensive and forced him to reply with a poem in the voice of his valet.) It stops Marot from writing anything else. It avoids discussion of charges against him—especially those accusing him of Lutheranism.

The fiction of the valet also allows a level of language inappropriate for the poet, such as name-calling, insults, and symbolic beating—a parody on the beatings noblemen had administered to their enemies. For this reason, one should beware of C.A. Mayer's assertion that Marot is naturally unchristian because of lines 219–20: "Enflez, vilain, que je me joue; / Sus, après, tournez l'autre joue" (Swell up villain, so that I can play / Get up, and afterwards, turn the other cheek).[14] It is Frippelippes, not Marot, saying these words.

The result is a judicious combination of realism and fantasy that comes to a head in the delightful onomatopoeia of the beating:

> Zon dessus l'oeil, zon sur le groin
> Zon sur le dos du Sagouin,
> Zon sur l'âne de Balaan!
> Ha! villain, vous pétez d'ahan:
> Le feu saint Antoine vous arde!
> Ça, ce nez, que je le nazarde,
> Pour t'apprendre avecques [*sic*] deux doigts
> A porter honneur où tu dois.
>
> (ll. 211–18)

(Zon on the eye, zon on the snout / Zon on the back of the Monkey, / Zon on the ass of Balaan! / Ha! villain, you burst out of fear: / May Saint Anthony's fire burn you / There, this nose, may I tweak it, / To teach you with two fingers / To be respectful where you should.)

P. M. Smith has studied the epistle's irony and parody.[15] For example, the title and the marginal notes of the poem that are interspersed with Latin make fun of scholastic commentaries and glosses. R. Griffin has pointed out, however, that despite the good fun, the poem is a serious satire in which Frippelippes puts down the literary rivals who attempted to usurp his master. At the same time, he assimilates Marot to David, the poet of the psalms (ll. 29–34).

In the epistle of Frippelippes, as in much of his poetry, therefore, we see Marot working hard to maintain the distance from events and issues appropriate to the sublime nature of his poetic calling. It was, however, to be the tragedy of his life that the mature fruits of his calling were never to be because his contract with power was too unstable to allow him to write unhindered. His last epistle (*Epîtres,* LVII) is addressed to the prince of the blood, François de Bourbon, but it is a final appeal to Francis I. There Marot promises that with the support of both king and prince he can become France's new Homer. Marot was to die a few months later in exile.

## Chants divers

Like the section "Complaints and Epitaphs" of the *Adolescence,* the section entitled *chants divers,* constitutes a transition between the longer poems (funeral poetry, elegies, epistles) and the shorter epitaphs of the "Cemetery." The word *chant,* which refers to a poem intended to be sung, is variously translated into English by "song," "canto," "carol," "hymn," "canticle," or "chant." We can discuss only the general features of the collection here. Marot's section is such a hodgepodge that Sebillet considers it the product of an editor's whim rather than Marot's own doing. [16] Its range includes ballades, long epigrams, free-form pieces in eight- or ten-line stanzas, *chants royaux,* and translations of Moschus's "Eros Drapetes" and of Petrarch's famous *canzone* "Standomi un giorno solo a la fenestra."

According to Sebillet, the model for all the forms is the *chant royal,* which he defines as a double ballade originally intended to be sung before kings or sung in honor of kings, immortal as well as mortal. [17] Thus the main criterion is the elevation of subject matter or audience. The style of these poems, however, is varied.

The most successful poems in the high style are Marot's epithalamia. The wedding song for Renée of Ferrara (*O.L.,* LXXXV) is the first epithalamium in French. The poem is an imitation of Catullus' epithalamium (poem 62) and like the eclogue for Louise de Savoie marks the pastiche kind of imitation characteristic of the Pléiade. Marot, however, attempts to achieve loftiness without speaking Greek in French as will the Pléiade. The title "Chant nuptial" (Wedding Song) is a domesticated French rendering of the Greek epithalamium. The elevated style of this poem may be seen in the frequent apostrophes (e.g., "O Nuit"), periphrases ("Fille du Roi," l. 31), capitalization, and epithets that precede the noun ("nobles Parents," l. 24).

The ballades and *chants royaux* of the collection are formal poems with a high-style ornament that use the Rhétoriqueur prosodic forms to their intended effect. These poems, however, are more "modern" than their counterparts in the *Adolescence*. Biblical allusions are scattered throughout that parallel Marot's pastiche-like imitation of the classics. Marot also handles neoclassical discourse more gracefully than in the *Adolescence* ballade celebrating the dauphin's birth (*O.D.*, LXXIII) with its awkward "Neptunus."

Often, however, the style of the poems is in a plain and neutral kind of French in terms of vocabulary and syntax. This includes the translations and Marot's moving "Cantique à la Déesse Santé" (Hymn to the Goddess of Health) (*O.L.*, LXXIX), which imitates Marcantonio Flaminio's neo-Latin "Hymnus in bonam valetudinem." The subject matter for the poem is lofty and prefigures Ronsard's encomiastic hymns to deities both in the hymns and in the odes. The seven stanzas imitated from Flaminio are an invocation that is at the same time an encomium of the goddess. The remaining stanzas are both a prayer and an encomium for Francis I. However, as J. Houston has observed in regards to the great *cantique* in which Marot describes Renée de Ferrara's sufferings at the hands of her husband (*O.L.*, LXXVI), the style in itself will not qualify for the high style in later European poetry.[18] It has virtually none of the kind of ornamentation we have seen in the epithalamium. Frequent capitalization is the only device that communicates loftiness.

At times, style stands in contrast to the content. The "Second *chant* d'amour fugitif" (*O.S.*, IV), for example, deals with elevated subjects and the immortals in a satirical low style that criticizes celibacy as unnatural. The final poem of the 1538 Section (*O.S.*, V) is a mock encomium on the court fool, Jean de Pichelin, that pokes fun at the high style. Consider, for example, the elevated vocabulary that Marot applies to the pretentious fool: "race," "Togue," "Règne," and Latinized place names: "Germanie" and "Gaul." This lighter touch is a device of closure that ends the section by taking a distance from the styles and subject matter it represents.

It also suggests that Marot never really excelled in the high style because he was too much aware of its ridiculousness. We have already seen how he mocks it in the epistle to the king he wrote after having been robbed. Given his place as the king's leading poet, it would seem that he reflects the court's preference for the "nonchalance" that Castiglione talks about. It was only with the advent of Henri II and his Medici wife that the high style would really come into its own in France.

## "Le Cimetière"

"Le Cimetière" (The Cemetery) is the *Suite's* collection of epitaphs. Its place is justified by the fact that it is the first section of short, free-form pieces; the epitaph, it should be recalled, is a funeral epigram traditionally written in a plain style. The epitaphs of "The Cemetery" deal with more important persons at court than those of the *Adolescence,* for Marot is now an official poet instead of a clerk. Poems in this section include those about Queen Claude, the Dauphin François, and various noble persons as well as court functionaries, poets (Crétin), and members of the royal household.

Marot's new station in life is translated into stiffer poetry. Here the traditional plainness of the genre borders on the uninteresting. The epitaphs of "The Cemetery" have less variety than those of the *Adolescence.* They are in general more flatly descriptive. Contrast, for example, the epitaph for Longueil (*O.D.,* XCI), which stands the topic of fame on its head with the more straightforward epitaph for Crétin (*O.D.,* CXIV). Written works of the departed are cause for mourning in the former epitaph, whereas in the latter they bring the more conventional consolation. Marot does at times, however, touchingly convey feelings about the dead in the manner of his earlier poems. Consider, for example, his pity for Queen Claude so in need of peace in a world of war (*O.D.,* CV), or his irony at the death of the king's mistress Madame de Châteaubriand (*O.D.,* CXXVIII).

The section is also less prosodically rich than its *Adolescence* counterpart, but there are some exceptions. The epitaph for Jan Cotereau is written in alexandrines, although it does not exploit the verse line's heroic potential to the full. Better is the long epitaph on Vuyart's horse (*O.D.,* CXXI) where Marot skillfully reproduces an impression of the horse's movements through rhyme and alliteration.

The epitaph for the horse is also an exception to the usual flat plainness of "The Cemetery." Like the *Chants divers* and the epitaphs of the *Adolescence,* the section ends with poems that mock their genre. In the 1533 *Suite* the epitaph for the horse ended "The Cemetery," and it possesses the same bittersweet quality as the epitaph for Jean Serre that concludes the epitaphs of the *Adolescence.* After touchingly evoking his own death, the horse tells us that his master will never let him be forgotten because he preferred mounting him to any "girl or woman." The 1538 *Suite* ends with two other satirical pieces that also depart from the usual manner. The first (*O.D.,* CXXIX) is an epitaph for Ortis, a Moorish attendant of Francis I. There Marot makes fun of his color. The second and last piece is a bawdy epitaph, "D'Alix" (*O.D.,* CXXII), which plays on the word *cul* (ass). The baseness of the epitaph is all the more surprising because the next section in the Dolet edition consists of Marot's translations of a series of the church's most important liturgical pieces.

## Oraisons (Prayers)

We have seen Marot juxtapose base and sublime before. The ballade that recounts Isabeau's denunciation precedes a *chant royal* on the conception of our lady. The "Temple of Cupid" in which the baptismal fonts are full of knights stroking naked ladies ends with a vision of Charity. Such contrasts are not at all unusual in the sixteenth century. We believe that they come from a hierarchical Neoplatonic vision of reality in which all experience is ranked on an ascending scale to God.

The oraisons (*T.,* 5) include translations of the Lord's Prayer, the Hail Mary, the Apostle's Creed, "Grace for a child," and Marot's translation of Psalm VI, which is the first of the penitential psalms. They were originally published in 1533 in Marguerite's *Miroir de l'Âme pécheresse* and reflect evangelist efforts to put the liturgy in the vernacular tongue. It is especially striking that Marot does not simply follow the Vulgate Latin of the New Testament passages, but takes into account the original Greek. He must have consulted specialists at Francis I's newly founded Collège de France. In general, despite the verse forms that necessitate occasional fillers, Marot's translations are of extremely good quality. They add virtually nothing to the age-old prayers. We shall consider such characteristics more in detail below in our description of the psalms, where Marot's talents as a translator bear their fullest fruits.[19]

## Chapter Nine

# The Final Sections of the 1538 Oeuvres: Epigrams, Ovid's *Metamorphoses*

## Marot's Epigrams

It is generally agreed that no French writer has ever equaled Marot's epigrams, which mark the debut of the genre in the language. The Pléiade shied away from competing with the master. It is probably out of jealousy that du Bellay unjustly insinuated that only the last line of poems in the genre were of interest. For Etienne Pasquier ranked Marot's epigrams along with the psalm translations as one of Marot's two claims to immortality.[1] The *précieux* poets tried to rival them. In the eighteenth century, Voltaire considered the epigram written for Semblançay the best in the French language. Even today many of Marot's epigrams seem to have been written in modern French. It is the plain style wit of the epigrams as well as of the epistles to which Boileau was referring with the expression *élégant badinage*. Although we have seen that there is much more in Marot's works, it is this aspect that transcended changes in fashions and presented a challenge to later writers.

Marot first published his epigrams in two books that come after the *Suite* in Dolet's 1538 edition. These will be the only ones we shall deal with in this study. They contain approximately half of Marot's total production. Other epigrams may be found in the Chantilly manuscript, in Marot's 1541 collection of *étrennes* (New Year's poems dedicated to various ladies at court), and in the posthumously published 1547 collection of epigrams imitated from Martial. The Dolet collection, however, is a fully representative example of Marot's art because it includes both *étrennes* and epigrams imitated from Martial. Yet it is impossible here to consider even the Dolet epigrams in detail. This chapter, therefore, concentrates (1) on the delicate balance of complicity and distance that Marot establishes in regards to his audience as a manifestation of the plain style and (2) on Marot's methods of imitation.

**Plain style complicity and distance.** The epigram is one of the classical plain-style poetic genres par excellence. It is a short poem originally intended to be an inscription—epitaphs are simply funeral epigrams—and it is noted for its tightness, concision, and wit. In the plain style, lucidity is a requirement as well.[2] The epigram also has a traditional link to the epistle. Martial, for example, calls his epigrams epistles. Like the epistles in the plain style, the epigram communicates the personality of the writer and assumes a common understanding between writer and audience. Yet the good epigrammatist also knows how to hold an audience at a respectful distance. Silences and gaps are just as important in this art as what is actually said. Along with lucidity and brevity, they are necessary qualities for a successful plain-style wit.

The Dolet epigrams have no readily apparent order. The first forty or so appeared in earlier editions of the *Adolescence* (*Les Dizains, blasons & envois*) and *Suite* (*Le Menu*). Marot lifted the groups in toto and renamed the poems epigrams. The rest of the some 250 poems seem to have no special arrangement. Thus it is best to classify them according to subject matter.

As a whole, the poems reflect the life of a poet at the court of Francis I. In the plain-style tradition, they celebrate the poet's membership in the refined elite associated with the court. As in the ballades, rondeaux, and epistles, there are requests scattered throughout the collection. Marot asks for the usual things: money, a horse, a confirmation of a money order, inscription in the rolls of the royal household. Marot wrote the following epigram at about the same time as Ballade V (*O.D.*, LXXI) discussed above and plays on the same expression—*coucher en l'état.* It is addressed to Montmorency:

> Quand par Acquits les gages on assigne,
> On est d'ennui tout malade & fâché;
> Mais à ce mal ne faut grand' médecine;
> Tant seulement faut être bien couché;
> Non pas en Lit, n'en Linge bien séché,
> Mais en l'Etat du noble Roi chrétien.
> Longtemps y a que debout je me tiens,
> Noble Seigneur; prenez doncques [*sic*] envie

> De me coucher à ce coup si très bien
> Que relever n'en puisse de ma vie.
>
> (*Epig.*, XXI)

(When wages are paid through money orders, / One is all sick and bothered by annoyances / But you do not need a lot of medicine for this illness; / As much as you need to be well bedded down / Not in Bed, nor in nice dry sheets, / But in the Household of the noble Christian King. / I have been standing for a long time, / Noble Lord; thus decide / To bed me down now so well / That I can never get up again [recover] for the rest of my life.)

The last line, which bears contradictory connotations in terms of illness or security, is a good example of the *pointe,* or condensed language, characteristic of the epigram. Its wit creates a distancing mask that permits Marot to ask for a life position at court in no uncertain terms, yet without saying it outright. This is not to say that the preceding lines of the epigram are worthless as du Bellay so unjustly claims. The everyday expressions such as *être bien couché* and the allusion to dry sheets are pleasant surprises along the way. They also give the poem an ease and familiarity typical of the plain style. At the same time allusions to the *noble Roi chrétien* and the *Noble Seigneur* despite the irony mark a clear distance. Although the ballade on the same expression has its merits, it seems wordy next to the concision and wit of this epigram. It is not difficult to see why Marot abandoned fixed-form poetry for the epigram later in life.

The "Mummery for Two Hermits" is an example of Marot's satirical epigrams, which include the epigram for Semblançay and the satirical contrast of the "beau" and "laid" *tétins.* The "Mummery" is a bawdy satire on both monastic life and love. As in the rondeau, the poet distances himself from passion through humor or intellectualizing, and it is interesting to compare the poem with the song about the hermit.

The song (*O.L.,* XLIII) is true to the laws of the genre, where passion controls reason and will. On the surface, the lover's hermitage is a renunciation of love, but clearly his intended prayers show that he has not yet recovered from his passion. His hermitage is portrayed as a symbol of his frustration rather than as a cure for it.

The "Mummery for Two Hermits," on the other hand, subordinates the passion of love to the will. (A mummery is a sort of pantomime.) There the hermits-to-be identify their passion with crude physical lust, which will go away with time and diet.

A. Le premier hermite

Savez-vous la raison pourquoi
Hors du monde je me retire
En un hermitage à recoi?
Sans faute je vous le veux dire.
Celle que tant j'aime & désire,
En lieu de me réconforter,
Toujours le cul arrière tire.
Le Diable la puisse emporter!

B. L'autre hermite

Je m'en vais tout vêtu de gris
En un bois; là je me confine
Au monde; aussi bien j'amaigris;
M'amie est trop dure ou trop fine!
Là vivrai d'eau & de racine;
Mais, par mon âme, il ne m'en chaut;
Cela me sera médecine
Contre mon mal qui est trop chaud.

(*Epig.*, C & CI)

(A. The First hermit / Do you know the reason why / Away from the world I withdraw / To a remote hermitage? / I shall certainly tell you. / She who I so love and desire, / Instead of comforting me, / Always backs her ass away. / The Devil take her! / B. The Other Hermit / I am going away all dressed in gray / To a wood; there I am confining myself / Away from the world; there I am going on a diet; / My friend is too hard or too refined! / There shall I live on water and roots; / But, by my soul, it does not matter to me; / It will be my medicine / Against my illness that is too heated.)

There are of course other reasons that the "mummery" is an epigram rather than a song. The two stanzas do not have the same rhyme scheme and so cannot be measured to the lyre. (Although the Mayer edition lists the two stanzas as two different epigrams, the 1538 Dolet edition I consulted prints them as stanzas a and b of the same epigram.)[3] They recall the original function of the epigram as an inscription, for they are meant to accompany the performance of the pantomime at court. We emphasize the differences in perspective, however, because we believe that Marot's poetic genres can be distinguished in terms of their discourse as well as their prosody.

The most famous of the satirical pieces is the celebrated epigram on Semblançay. Here plain-style wit and concision balance value judgments against careful silences to create a masterpiece of praise and condemnation.

> Lorsque Maillard, Juge d'enfer, menait
> À Montfaucon Semblançay l'âme rendre
> À votre avis lequel des deux tenait
> Meilleur maintien? Pour le vous faire entendre,
> Maillard semblait homme qui mort va prendre
> Et Semblançay fut si ferme vieillard
> Que l'on cuidait (pour vrai) qu'il menât pendre
> À Montfaucon le Lieutenant Maillard.
>
> (*Epig.*, XLIII)

(When Maillard, Judge of Hell, led / Semblançay to render his soul at Montfaucon / In your opinion which of the two had / A better demeanor? In case you don't understand, / Maillard seemed the man who was going to his death / And Semblançay was such a steady old man / That one thought (really) that he was leading to be hung / At Montfaucon Lieutenant Maillard.)

The interrogations and clarifying asides are the principal devices of plain style, but in truth Marot's poem defies interpretation. The poet may not like Maillard and admire Semblançay, but he speaks only of appearances. We think that the poem is carefully constructed to appeal to both parties at court. Those who thought Semblançay innocent could interpret appearances as reality. Those who thought him guilty could denounce the false appearance.[4]

By far the greatest number of poems are written to the ladies at court. The presence of ladies outside the immediate royal family was a novelty at the time. It represented a whole new conception of life at court. Marot celebrates women's beauty and wisdom. Marguerite is a "monster"; she has a "Feminine body, the Heart of a man and the Head of an Angel" (*Epig.*, IV, l. 10). In Epigram

III it is perfectly clear that we are to consider Madame Jeanne Gaillarde more beautiful than Helen. Yet with exquisite plain-style silence, Marot never mentions the Greek woman's name:

Other poems of this group re-create the conversations that must have gone on in royal quarters. Marot philosophizes with Marguerite de Navarre: "Nous fûmes, sommes & serons" (We were, are and shall be; *Epig.*, CXXXI). Elsewhere he writes an epigram for Hélène de Tournon for having lost a parlor game (*Epig.*, LXXXVII) that is comparable to the epistle he wrote to Madame de Pons (*Epîtres*, XXXVIII). It generates a brief exchange between him and Marguerite de Navarre. The only money he can pay with, he tells Hélène de Tournon, will be poetry. Marguerite answers saying that his money is worth a thousand times regular money, and Marot replies in the following epigram that is a masterpiece of plain-style complicity and distancing. Such procedures as the play on titles plainly suggests without directly saying it that Marot and Marguerite share an aristocratic disdain for the bourgeoisie. ("Sire" is a title that one addresses to superiors; "Monsieur" one uses for equals.)[5] At the same time, however, Marot subtly pokes fun at Marguerite's royal stance above money by showing how her little poem is really worth more than gold:

> Mes créanciers, qui de Dixains n'ont cure,
> Ont lu le vôtre, & sur ce leur ai dit:
> Sire Michel, sire Bonaventure,
> La soeur du Roi a pour moi fait ce dit.
> Lors eux, cuidant que fusse en grand crédit,
> M'ont appelé monsieur à cri & cor,
> Et m'a valu votre écrit autant qu'or;
> Car promis ont, non seulement d'attendre,
> Mais d'en prêter (foi de marchand) encore;
> Et j'ai promis (foi de Clément) d'en prendre.
>                                        (*Epig.*, LXXXVIII)

(My creditors, who don't care about Dixains, / Read yours, and I said to them: / Sir Michael, Sir Bonaventure, / The sister of the King wrote this for me. / Then they, believing that I had a lot of credit, / Called me "monsieur" with cries and trumpets, / And your poem was worth as much as gold to me; / Because they promised, not only to wait, / But to even lend (on the faith of merchants) more; / And I promised (on the faith of Clément) to avail myself of their offer.)

*Etrennes* scattered throughout evoke New Year's Day celebrations. Marot's masterpiece in this genre is of course the collection he published separately in 1541 under the title *Les Étrennes de Clément Marot*. It is a string of pieces that prefigures the famous *guirlandes* of the *précieux* poets and also the poems about nothing of Mallarmé and the symbolists. The *étrennes* of the 1538 edition have a great deal of variety. An example of the lighter vein is a little note written to a demoiselle. The sudden reversal of realities at the end is a good example of the epigrammatist's *pointe*. Its wit depends on the creation of a sudden momentary distance between the poet and the lady:

> Demoiselle que j'aime bien,
> Je te donne pour la pareille
> Tes étrennes d'un petit Chien
> Qui n'est pas plus grand que l'Oreille.
> Il jappe, il mord, il fait merveille;
> Il va déjà tout seul trois pas;
> C'est pour toi que je l'appareille,
> Excepté que je ne l'ai pas.
>
> (*Epig.*, XV)

(Damsel that I like a lot, / I give you in lieu of / Your New Year's gift a little Dog / That is no bigger than the Ear. / It barks, it bites, it is marvelous; / It can already do three steps alone; / It is for you that I am getting it ready / Except that I do not have it.)

Contrast to this poem the more learned fourteen-line *étrenne* (*Epig.*, XI) that features a little mythological narrative on how roses became red. It falls outside of the scope of the present chapter but should be mentioned as a fourteen-line poem that is not a sonnet. (Marot is a candidate for having written the first sonnet in French.) Marot's elevated encomium (*O.D.*, CLXXIX) to the governor of Lyon, Pomponio Trivulce, which appeared among the epigrams in 1538, however, does skillfully exploit the possibilities of the sonnet form.

The overwhelming number of poems dedicated to women is devoted to love. Most of these are dedicated to Anne d'Alençon, related to Marguerite's first husband through a bastard line. Their subject matter represents a wide range. Like the satirical epigrams and the rondeaux, these serious love epigrams also distance passion with wit and humor. A good example is the famous snow epigram. Here the

Petrarchan play on fire and ice is an intellectual game that contrasts
to the more direct cry from the heart in the songs:

> Anne (par jeu) me jeta de la Neige
> Que je cuidais froide certainement;
> Mais c'était feu, l'expérience en ai-je;
> Car embrasé je fus soudainement.
> Puis que le feu loge secrètement
> Dedans la Neige, où trouverai-je place
> Pour n'ardre point? Anne, ta seule grâce
> Eteindre peut le feu que je sens bien,
> Non point par Eau, par Neige ni par Glace
> Mais par sentir un feu pareil au mien.
>
> (*Epig.*, XXIV)

(Anne (as a game) threw on me some Snow / That I believed most
certainly cold; / But it was fire, I know what it is; / Because I was suddenly
all aflame with it. / Since fire lodges secretly / In Snow, where will I find
a place / Not to burn? Anne, your grace alone / Can put out the fire that
I feel so well, / Not by Water, by Snow nor by Ice / But by feeling a fire
similar to mine.)

The subtlety of the poem escapes critics intent on upholding the
image of shallow Marotic banter rather than listening to the depths
of silence behind his deceptively plain-speaking juggling of complicity with distance. It is true that there is an atmosphere of easy
familiarity suggested by the game-playing fun and the poet's mention of the Lady's name, but critics go too far in assuming that
Marot is playing the game too. He never says that he is. Rather
Anne's little game leads to the poet's suffering and cry for grace.
The true subtlety of the poem is that the playful fire and ice works
thinly to mask the implication that the game is a one-sided one.

**Two forms of imitation.**   In contrast to the rondeaux that are
clearly of Petrarchan inspiration, Marot's so-called Petrarchan epigrams play a kind of Petrarchan hide-and-go-seek. The thirty-five
epigrams of this group repeat only commonplace conventions such
as the antithesis between fire and ice. It is true that Marot mentions
Laura, Petrarch's beloved, several times in the course of the collection, and in the Petrarchan tradition he dedicates the second
book to Anne. Yet to call a poem Petrarchan simply because of an
image or convention is most dangerous because Petrarchan and

French medieval conventions of love are virtually indistinguishable. This is especially the case because of Marot's practice of free and creative imitation. He assimilates a poem completely and re-creates a new entity that seems entirely natural in French. Thus it is impossible to say whether Marot is naturalizing a foreign convention or simply continuing a national one.

For example, J. Vianey considers the blasons for the *beau* and *laid tétins* in the style of the Italian *strambotti*.[6] Yet, the blason is a well-established genre in medieval poetry. For the contrast between beautiful and ugly, one need go no further than François Villon's "Belle Heaulmière." Elsewhere, when Marot alludes to Mademoiselle d'Albret's *gorge d'Albâtre* or to Diana's "bouche de corail" (*Epig.*, LI & CII), he is at best adding a slight Petrarchan touch to a firmly established French tradition.

Marot's use of the eight-line stanza also recalls the *strambotti*, but he uses it in an entirely French medieval manner that recalls Villon more than Italy.[7] On the other hand, the epigrams dealing with departures and arrivals or the poems dealing with kisses belong to the Latin elegiac tradition, and in the case of the *étrenne* on the rose, the myth comes straight out of the rhetorician Aphthonius's *Progymnasmata*. The blatantly Petrarchan snow epigram closely imitates, in fact, an epigram by Petronius.[8] Nevertheless, we do not go so far as R. Griffin in suggesting that it is better to name the conventions than to identify their source.[9] Nor do we agree entirely with C. A. Mayer that Marot was more Petrarchan before his trip to Italy than after.[10] Rather, we see in this pervasive yet elusive Petrarchan presence in the epigrams an imperative of the witty concision characteristic of the genre. In the rondeaux Marot imitates specific Petrarchan poems; in the epigrams he plays a little game of Petrarchism that hides Petrarchism. "Petrarch? Why I was only following Aphthonius and imitating Petronius," we hear him say with a smile.

In fact, the Petrarchism is indirect probably because Marot conceived of the epigram as a classical genre. Even though he wrote some of these poems before he called them epigrams, scholars usually agree that he conceived of them in the antique manner. Sebillet, for example, treats Marot's epigrams as imitated from Greek and Latin. Greek epigrams are brought together in the *Greek Anthology* which Marot probably did not read, but there is an

unmistakable Latin influence that includes Martial, Catullus, Petronius, and Renaissance neo-Latin poets. In these cases, we have
an imitation that approaches the line-by-line pastiches of the Pléiade.
The last two lines of the snow epigram, as Petrarchan as they may
seem, closely imitate Petronius.[11] Yet Marot in contrast to the
Pléiade always naturalizes and adapts to a French reality. In the
snow epigram, he adds the idea of the little one-sided game that
evokes the playful atmosphere reigning at the court of Francis I.

The most important of the authors Marot was to imitate is
Martial, not so much in the 1538 edition as elsewhere. Marot
offered several epigrams in imitation of Martial in the Chantilly
manuscript, and Marnef Brothers published a posthumous edition
of them in 1547. Marot's epistolary plain-style conception of the
epigram is, as we have seen, directly inherited from Martial. In
addition, the Gryphius 1538 edition had three epigrams imitated
from Martial. There is an epigram addressed to Mellin de St. Gelais
(*Epig.*, LXXX) and the two that replaced the one dedicated to
Dolet (*Epig.*, XLIX and L). Marot adapts Martial to French just as
he does Petronius.[12] Consider, for example, the epigram to Mellin
de St. Gelais:

> Ta Lettre (Mellin) me propose
> Qu'un gros sot en rime compose
> Des vers par lesquels il me point.
> Tiens-toi sûr qu'en rime n'en {*sic*} prose
> Celui n'écrit aucune chose
> Duquel l'ouvrage on ne lit point.

(Your Letter (Mellin) tells me / That a fat fool composes in rhyme /
Verses by which he attacks me. / Be assured that neither in rhyme nor
in prose / He writes nothing / Who's work one does not read.)

Marot's French version is longer as seems to be a necessity of
the language. Compare the Latin, "Versiculos in me narratur scribere Cinna / non scribit, cuius carmina nemo legit" (Cinna is said
to write verses against me. He doesn't write at all whose poems
no one reads, 3, 9). Marot, however, subtly re-creates the impression of the original. Although he loses the concise "scribere . . .
/ non scribit" of the Latin, he gives an equivalent in the play "rime
compose" / "rime n'en prose." This opposition, by the way, also

recalls one of the great differences between French and Latin. The latter does not use rhyme in poetry. Marot carries this way of adapting equivalences in French to a fine art in his translation of the psalms, and he expresses a sensitivity to the problem in the preface to his translation of Ovid's *Metamorphoses*, book I.

## Book I of Ovid's *Metamorphoses*

**A philosophy of translation.** Marot first published this translation (*T.*, VII) separately with E. Roffet in 1534 and read parts of it to Francis I as early as 1526. Although his preface contains a philosophy of translation that seems to prefigure the Pléiade, he in fact outlines a program for a kind of adaptation that is far more respectful of French even though it introduces the luster of antiquity. Marot says that he came upon the *Metamorphoses* while seeking out something "high" (*haut*) to translate for the king because his own poetry was too "low" (*bas*). He goes on to say that he attempted with all his might to reproduce (*contrefaire*) Ovid's manner so that those who do not know Latin could understand how he wrote and see the difference between the ancients and the moderns. He also observes that the names of the Greek gods such as Apollo and Daphne could decorate French just as they did Latin and that even Ovid's title, *metamorphosis*, is a Greek word signifying "transformation."[13]

Marot's translation, however, avoids the Pléiade's unsettling habit of speaking Greek and Latin in French. Although Marot does keep proper names and the Greek-inspired title, he avoids neologisms and a Latinate syntax. The resulting naturalness of Marot's French reproduces the impression of Ovid's manner, which Marot characterizes as *doux*. The term belongs to a long Western tradition going back to the Greek *glaphuros* meaning "smooth" or "sweet" as opposed to "harsh" or "austere." It was associated with the high-style epic and later sixteenth-century attempts to rise above the middle style in love lyrics that we now call "mannerist."[14] Marot's translation is a French equivalent of Ovid's flowing middle style. The contrast between this style and the lofty subject matter suggests the kind of precedent Marot must have had in mind for others of his poems with an elevated subject matter but a clear and natural style.

**A fitting conclusion to the 1538 edition.** The extraordinary length of the *Metamorphoses* doubtlessly justifies its place at the end of the 1538 edition. However, it also contrasts to the opening works of the edition, which are arranged in careful hierarchical order; despite Ovid's lofty subject matter, his theme is the upsetting of all hierarchy and order through transformation. Although the poem begins with a description of how Chaos was ordered to make the universe, its main themes are degradation and transformation. It evoked four ages of history, each worse than its predecessor: gold, silver, bronze, and iron. Humanity is destroyed by the deluge and then re-created out of stone. Several other beings are transformed. Daphne, for example, is changed into a tree. Thus the 1538 edition that begins with careful attention to rank and formality ends with an evocation of the contingencies and changes that undermine form.

## Chapter Ten
# Marot's Psalm Translations

Marot's psalm translations are one of his principal claims to fame. Etienne Pasquier, for example, considered them along with the epigrams as one of his two major achievements.[1] Peletier said that they were odes in fact if not in name.[2] Indeed, these translations were meant to be sung. They observe the alternation between masculine and feminine rhymes, and, in the group of forty-nine psalms, forty-one different strophic forms are based on popular rhythms akin to those of the songs we have seen. They represent no less than the beginning of modern French prosody.[3] Ronsard admits to having used them to write his odes. They were set to music by the best composers of the time and spread like wildfire. (Unfortunately we cannot deal with the music in this study, but the Goudimel settings are still appealing.) Jean Calvin's nascent French reformed church used them for liturgical purposes and many a French Protestant martyr died with them on his or her lips. Their effect must have been a cross between gospel songs and the new simple but decorous English of parts of the 1976 American Episcopal *Book of Common Prayer*.

The 1538 edition does not throw any light on the psalm translations because they were not published until between 1539 and 1543. The principal editions were published by Roffet in 1541 and 1543. Another edition that formed the basis of the Constantin edition was published without indication of place or publisher in 1543.[4] In the biographical chapter, we have already dealt with the fact that the court, rather than Calvinist loyalties, was the inspiration for the psalms; Marot's Calvinist connection was due to force of circumstance. Thus we shall concentrate on Marot's development of a sublime low style and his translation of Hebrew form as well as content. The latter represents a new, close kind of imitation, parallel to what he practices in the epigrams.

## A Sublime Low Style

Marot's characterization of the psalms' level of style in the dedicatory epistles to the king and to the ladies of France is contradictory. In the former (*T.*, pp. 309–14), he speaks of them as if they are in the highest of styles. He says that Homer did not do better (ll. 115–16), that David's poems are "decorated" with more rhetorical figures than Francis I's crown (ll. 119–26), and that David the eagle flies higher than Horace the alouette (ll. 129–32). In the epistle to the ladies of France (*T.*, pp. 314–16), on the other hand, Marot dreams of a time when common farmers, tradesmen, and shepherds will sing psalms and canticles to soothe them in their daily tasks. Both positions have ample Christian precedent. Marot's comparisons between David, Homer, and Horace belong to a long tradition opposing the virtues of Greek, Latin, and Hebrew poetry. Marot's vision of a working persons' psalms echoes Jerome.[5] The contradiction comes from a clash between the Judeo-Christian and Greco-Roman traditions. Although it is not appropriate to consider the Hebrew psalms as well as much of the rest of the Bible in terms of the classical hierarchy of styles, biblical poetry seems to belong to the lower end of the spectrum.[6] There exists in the biblical tradition an ideal of sublime lowness. The Supreme Being expresses Himself humbly so to be accessible to everyone.

Humanists in France before 1550 wrote simply so as to reach a wide public. The religious writers among them returned to this early Christian simplicity. After 1550, culture was to be controlled by an elite that held the *vulgaire* in contempt and worked to elevate the style of French.[7] Religious poetry from this perspective was written in a neoclassical high style that has little biblical flavor.

Unfortunately most post-Renaissance critics judge Marot's translations through the colored glasses of this elitist, neoclassical high style. Voltaire laughs at their inappropriateness and pedantry. He considers Marot's translation of Psalm 68 ("Que Dieu se montre seulement") as fit to be sung by lecherous bodyguards.[8] (Voltaire, let us remember, considered Shakespeare an uneven genius whose plays were in part too shocking for the Parisian stage.) Twentieth-century scholars reproach the psalms for a uniform "grayness" and "absence of style": they accuse Marot of not distinguishing between words of the vocabulary according to their degree of nobility or triviality, and they find his popular rhythms contradictory to the meaning.[9] This criticism is to be expected. The French language has been so thoroughly reshaped according to a neoclassical model that the level of Marot's vocabulary will seem incongruous even to the best intentioned of us. We cannot undo four hundred years of history. The perception of an "absence of style," however, comes from a prejudice that refuses to accord Hebrew stylistic devices any status. Marot's psalm translations are plain in that they adopt popular rhythms, use a simple vocabulary, and eschew the devices of classical rhetoric. Yet in distinction to the conversational plain style he creates in the epigrams and better known verse epistles, Marot in the psalm translations creates a low style that is gracefully ornamented with the sublime yet simple figures of David, "more numerous than the gems in Francis I's crown."

## David's Ornaments

Ô notre Dieu & seigneur amiable
Combien ton nom est grand & admirable
Par tout ce val terrestre & spacieux
Qui ta puissance élève sur les cieux.

En tout se voit ta grand' vertu parfaite,
Jusque [*sic*] à la bouche aux enfants qu'on allaite,
Et rends par la confus & abbatu
Tout ennemi qui nie ta vertu.

Mais quand je vois & contemple en courage
Tes cieux qui sont de tes doigts haut ouvrage,
Etoiles, lune & signes différents
Que tu as faits & assis en leurs rangs,

Adonc je dis, à part moi, ainsi comme
Tout ébahi, & qu'est-ce-que de l'homme,
D'avoir daigné de lui te souvenir
Et de vouloir en ton soin le tenir?

Tu l'as fait tel que plus il ne lui reste
Fors être Dieu (car tu l'as quant du reste)
Abondamment de gloire environné,
Rempli de biens & d'honneur couronné.

Régner le fais sur les oeuvres tant belles
De tes deux mains comme seigneur d'icelles;
Tu as (de vrai), sans quelque exception,
Mis sous ses pieds tout en subjection.

Brebis & boeufs & leurs peaux & leurs laines,
Tous les troupeaux des hauts monts & des plaines,
En général toutes bêtes cherchants
À pâturer par les bois & les champs.

Oiseaux de l'air qui volent & qui chantent
Poissons de mer, ceux qui nagent & hantent
Par les sentiers de mer grands & petits,
Tu les as tous à l'homme assujettis.

Ô notre Dieu & seigneur amiable,
Comme à bon droit est grande [sic] & admirable
L'excellent bruit de ton nom précieux
Par tout ce val terrestre & spacieux. [10]

Although it has been our practice to translate all French verse
passages, in this case, any translation would so distort Marot's translation that we have decided to give a modern translation from the
Hebrew psalm itself: (Asterisks mark Hebrew lines that modern
editors either consider uncertain or comment upon.)

*For the leader; on the *gittith*. A Psalm of David.

2 O Lord, our Lord,
How majestic is Your name throughout the earth,
*You who have covered the heavens with Your splendor!*

3 *From the mouths of infants and sucklings
You have founded strength on account of Your foes,
to put an end to enemy and avenger.*

4 When I behold Your heavens, the work of Your fingers,
the moon and stars that You set in place,

5 what is man that You have been mindful of him,
mortal man that You have taken note of him,

6 that You have made him little less than *divine,*
and adorned him with glory and majesty;

7 You have made him master over Your handiwork,
laying the world at his feet,

8 sheep and oxen, all of them,
and wild beasts, too;

9 the birds of the heavens, the fish of the sea,
whatever travels the paths of the seas.

10 O Lord, our Lord, how majestic is Your name throughout the earth![11]

As we have said in our chapter on Marot's life, the poet probably did not read Hebrew, even though he claims to be closer to it than his predecessors in the title of the Roffet editions and in the dedicatory epistle to the king. Pasquier asserts that he worked with Vatable, but modern critics believe that to mean a few consultations and perhaps attendance in Vatable's courses. Marot most probably worked with new French and Latin translations by persons who knew Hebrew. His most important sources were Olivetan's French translation of the Bible and Bucer's Latin translation, but not Lefèvre's French translation. M. Jeanneret observes that Marot's variants show an ever increasing closeness to Hebrew and submits that they reflect a close collaboration with Calvin.[12]

Marot's achievement is most striking for its sensitive handling of the inevitable distortions that result from any rhymed stanzaic translation. The poem is written in quatrains, one of the favorite forms of modern French poetry. Its stanzaic form is necessary for singing. Yet there is a correspondence between Hebrew verse and stanzaic unit. Here the ten stanzas correspond to the ten Hebrew verses. Of course, the stanza is larger than the Hebrew verse, so Marot is obliged to fill out the original. Consider, however, how Hebrew verse 10 repeats only half of verse 1. Marot, who cannot cut a stanza in half, instead reworks material in the first stanza so that line 4, which corresponds to the words the Hebrew leaves out, is not repeated in stanza 10, whereas line 3, which corresponds to the end of the Hebrew verse, now comes at the end. Furthermore, although the last stanza must repeat in four lines what the first did in only three, Marot manages to remain very close to the Hebrew. His fillers have negligible doctrinal content; rather, they draw out implications of the original. "Comme à bon droit" is an approving way of saying "combien". "Le bruit de ton nom" is a restriction to the sense of

hearing that we do not see in the English translation, and it recalls
the Renaissance theme of fame. Yet it remains close to the Olivetan
1535 translation and to the Vulgate, both of which introduce the
notion of praise. With an elitist's disdain for simplicity, scholars
have criticized these fillers as anodyne and boring, but they play
the double role of faithfully reflecting the original while unobtru-
sively completing the verse lines.

Marot's faithfulness to the text in terms of what French verse
structure will sustain is all the more striking, given the prevalent
tendencies of the times either to allegorize or to Christianize. Marot
never translates for purposes of doctrine. While subsequent editions
have variants that reflect the influence of Calvin, a reader of Hebrew,
Marot's psalms do not have a Calvinist doctrinal slant. Most often
his errors are those of Olivetan and Bucer rather than his own. The
controversial lines 13–14 constitute a striking illustration of this.
They say that God has made man so that nothing remains "except
to be God." This is one of only two passages in all the forty-nine
psalms that Marot's archenemy Artus Désiré branded as heretical,
because the Vulgate reads *paulo minus ab angelis* ("little less than the
angels"). Yet, both Olivetan and Bucer translate "God" or "Gods,"
so that Marot's translation shows the influence of the then latest
opinion of Hebraicists. (It is interesting to note that this is a passage
that provokes comment in modern editions such as the Jewish Publication Society's translation above and the Jerusalem Bible.) The
expression is changed to "god or angel" only in editions used in the
reformed church, but in neither of the Roffet editions.

With an art that hides art, Marot admirably reproduces the salient
characteristics of Hebrew poetry in a language completely unsuited
to them. French is more given to abstraction, subordination, and
a marshaling of phrases according to logic and cadence. The Hebrew
of the psalms on the other hand is full of parataxis, parallelism,
repetitions and pleonasm. These very devices are the essence of their
"lowness" for the neoclassical elitist, their sublimity for the religious
humanist. Marot admirably attempts to reproduce these characteristics without violating the nature of French. For example, as M.
Jeanneret has observed, when Marot does put in conjunctions, he
never breaks into a Hebrew unit. Rather, he uses conjunctions to
join sentences (in this case, stanzas III and IV) which correspond to
Hebrew verses.[13] Compare also lines 14–16 with the Hebrew original. Marot does not translate "son of Man" here as he does in the

variants and as do the translations he used. He does, however, keep the parallelism "mindful of" / "taken note of." Furthermore, he does not keep the doubling "infants and sucklings," but his use of "jusqu'à" has precedent in Olivetan and Bucer, and he does keep the more concrete of the two expressions.

The genitive construction, "son of man," is a typical kind of Hebraicism that Marot uses frequently elsewhere in his translations. We do not find another Hebraicism he often uses: the singular for a couple (e.g., "eye" for "eyes"), because it is not retained in the translations he consulted. However, his feeling for the specificity of Hebrew is so great that his interpolations often take on the stamp of the original. Consider, for example, the filler "grands et petits" (l. 31) that sounds like a Hebrew couplet. Consider also the expression "val terrestre" which the modern Hebrew translates simply as "throughout the earth," but that the Vulgate translates as "universa terra" and Olivetan as "terre universelle." Here Marot replaces the abstract "universal" with a more Hebraically concrete synecdoche. Furthermore, the expression not only recalls such Hebrew expressions as "vale of tears" but also belongs to the register of pastoral poetry. Thus Marot eschews the high style for the low in this category of sublime of poetry. Again we see his original poetic genius subtly making use of unexpected means to high creative ends.

Marot is also sensitive to the Hebrew portraiture of God. The first line brings up the whole problem of God's name. There are two traditions of translation for the first line. One tradition says some variant of "Lord our lord." The other tradition, which Olivetan, Bucer, and thus Marot follow, says a variant of "Jehovah our Lord." Marot also does not shy away from low style anthropomorphisms in references to God's fingers and hands.

We have not exhausted the richness of Marot's translations. Their so-called inappropriateness is a product of changes in the French language. For example, the word *amiable* may seem inappropriate to modern ears, but it could well have suggested the Neoplatonic theories of love we have seen in the dedicatory epistle to the ladies of France. Instead of "grayness," however, we see a controlled, yet accessible sobriety of a sublime low style. As both O. Douen and M. Jeanneret have amply demonstrated, no French writer has ever been able to equal Marot, be it Malherbe, Bertaut, Racine, or Lamartine. Bèze, who was as concerned with an accurate translation as Marot, was unable to re-create the Hebrew form. Gone are the parallelisms, correspondence between Hebrew verse and stanza, and careful use of conjunctions and concrete language. Others, such as Malherbe (compare his paraphrase of Psalm VIII) and Bertaut, write in a more elevated style, but they change the meaning and lose that creative conflict between sublimity and lowness that Marot reproduces so well in his translation of David's ornaments.

## Chapter Eleven

# Marot's Religion in Major Poems outside the 1538 Edition

As we already have seen, Marot's poems in the 1538 edition, including his attacks on Rome and monasticism, do not go beyond the nonschismatic reforming tendencies of the French court.[1] Critics in general agree that the same is true for the rest of Marot's poetry except for his satire on justice, "Hell," the great epistle he wrote to Francis I from Ferrara, and the poems of dubious authenticity written during his second exile. These just mentioned poems, which appear outside of the 1538 edition, deserve closer consideration.

The first two, like the epistle to Bouchard, have received considerable critical attention because they contain very slippery and ironic declarations of faith. They are poles apart from the poems of doubtful authenticity, which are heavy-handed doctrinal pronouncements that prompted C. d'Héricault to say that Marot, who began as an almost pedantic poet, died as a preacher-poet.[2]

We have seen in the epistle to Bouchard that Marot assumes a stance that identifies with court evangelism and its pretensions of establishing a syncretic religious reform that would include Rome, the reformers, and indeed other religions. We believe Marot never abandoned this ideal and for that reason never openly attacked any group except to deny his membership in it. His defenses appear slippery to us because in the plain-style tradition they are filled with silences intended to be understood by an in-group. The tragedy of which Marot was insufficiently aware is that the political situation had changed so rapidly that the silences meant to defend him condemned him instead.

## "L'Enfer"

In this, his longest poem (O.S., I), Marot says that he writes about the hellish prison of Châtelet now that he can see it from the safe distance of the relatively pleasant quarters at Chartres. He traces events from his girlfriend Luna's accusation that he broke Lent to his defense before the judge. We see him enter the prison, observe different legal procedures, lawsuits, and the use of torture on others before he appears in front of the judge to present his own case.

The initial descriptions and observations (ll. 21–303) contain a full-fledged satire on justice. Marot's criticisms, however, fall almost entirely within the range of traditional medieval satire on justice. He denounces procedures that favor the big and rich, the double talk of legal jargon, and the tendency of lawsuits to drag on and multiply like serpents from Hydra's head. The most original touch of this satire is his condemnation of torture. Montaigne is the only other writer in the century to have denounced the practice.[3] Marot blames all of these abuses on the poor preaching of the Christian clergy; he accuses them of allowing society to forget the true meaning of Christian charity.

Following line 303, Marot presents his own defense. He puts forth his station as a man of the court and states his name. He cannot be Lutheran, he says ironically, because he has the same first name as the Pope Clement—the pope with the power to conquer Hell. His last name, Marot, resembles Virgil's, Maro. Although Marot admits that he is not a Maro, he expresses hope in the new Maecenas (the cardinal of Lorraine) and launches into a full-scale praise of the Renaissance of letters in France. Then he tells how he was born in Cahors before he came north to France and the court where he learned French. Now he is a valet de chambre for Marguerite. After the king is free, Marot predicts she will liberate him.

The poem is full of literary reminiscence and allusion. Marot's arrest after the denunciation of his mistress as well as his criticism of the pope's power to conquer the devils of hell with a stole ("étole," l. 354) hark back to Villon's *Testament* and "Ballade en vieil langage français." His vision of hell guarded by Cerberus recalls Virgil and Dante, but more immediately, Lemaire's "Second Epître de l'amant vert," his "Cortège de Vénus," and his *Illustrations de Gaule*. Marot's description of the serpents springing from Hydra's head and his use of mythology in general (e.g., the reference to "Hymnides," l. 328) is also reminiscent of Lemaire. Virgil's eclogues also drift through Marot's descriptions of Cahors and of the pastoral gods at court.

**An ornamented low-style satire.**   Traditionally, in the classical hierarchy, satire is a plain-style genre par excellence. "Hell," on the other hand, is highly ornamented, but it is a mistake to hold it up to a neoclassical standard of "eloquent satire."[4] Marot, rather, writes a low-style poem that ironically incorporates elements of higher-style poetry into the game. This approach is much like the ballades. Characteristics of the low style are Marot's rather direct syntax, acute sense of picturesque detail, and occasional notes of personal veracity.[5] The poem's loose composition is another characteristic of a low style. It is not a well-planned epic—in contrast to Dante's *Inferno*—or a Ciceronian oration, but rather a satire. The mythological imagery and allegory account for the elevated ornamentation of the poem. Modern critics who call them inappropriate, awkward attempts at formality do not seize the ironic effects of the clash between high and low.[6]

Consider, for example, the ironic address to the Judge Rhadamanthys. A satirical piece in which allegory and mythology express the poet's mocking scorn for his adversaries, it is distinctly lower than the careful, formal addresses in "The Judgment of Minos." Here Marot continues to work out the allegorical system of the poem. If Châtelet is Hell, then the court is Olympus. (The analogy also mirrors court fashion that dressed the royal family and the nobility in the guise of Olympian deities.) Marot characterizes Marguerite as a wise "Pallas" (ll. 321–22) and Francis I as Jupiter and protector of "letters and the lettered" who will bring about a Renaissance of learning (ll. 367–76). He figuratively evokes the lords and ladies at court as the lesser deities (ll. 326–35). One can imagine the effect of such language as Marot read the poem to Francis I and the court. It is complimentary yet playful. We see a smile as Marot gives the language of court propaganda a new twist: if "we" who live with the king belong to the "Angelic souls" of Heaven, then "they" of Châtelet are the "Plutonic souls" of Hell. This, by the way, is not the only time that Marot uses the official discourse ironically. Note also the epistle that he later wrote to the king on having been robbed (*Epîtres,* XXV, ll. 123–30.).

Critics judge the satire of "Hell" inferior to Rabelais's portraits because it does little more than repeat commonplaces of medieval satire without going into much detail.[7] They do not, however, sufficiently reckon with such an artful juxtaposition of low style with high, nor do they take into account the necessary economy of poetry in relation to prose. Although Rabelais is a master of language, his medium gives him more room for detail. Marot is a true poet whose message exists not so much in the content of his words as in the artistic weight he gives them.

**Religion of a courtier.** Marot's playfulness is more evident in the coy silence—similar to that of the epistle to Bouchard—that he maintains in his declaration of faith. His defense of his religious orthodoxy on the basis of the name he shares with Clement VII ironically mocks straightforward arguments and is obviously intended for an in-group.[8] Confident that Francis I and Marguerite will liberate him (ll. 304–40, and ll. 417–88), he refuses even so much as to enter into discussion with the judges in hell.

The real note of seriousness in the poem comes not only from Marot's attack on Châtelet but also in his characterization of himself as a poet. Marot concludes the list of people at court by evoking those who know him best:

> Mais par sus tout suis connu des neuf Muses,
> Et d'Apollo, Mercure & tous leurs fils
> En vrai amour & science confits.
>
> (ll. 336–38)

(But above all I am known by the nine Muses, / And by Apollo, Mercury and all of their sons / Steeped in true love and science.)

Contrast also how Marot explains his calling as a poet much more seriously than his religious affiliation. Although he flippantly uses the common name he shares with Pope Clement VII to assert an identity of religious conviction in defense of accusations of Lutheranism, he dares not force the similarity between Marot and Maro into an identity of poetic talent. Marot writes his satire on the pope and justice from a position "above" both canon and secular law, bowing only before his king and poetic model. Thus Marot is not, as Jourda maintains, disrespectful of "Power" and "powers."[9] Rather, he is disrespectful of the "powers" of justice and of the papacy, because he identifies with the "Power" of the royal court.

We have already considered the "hermeneutics of censorship" at work behind such a passage in our discussion of the epistle to Bouchard. Although this ornamented low-style poem differs from the plain style of the epistle, the use of silence as a wink of complicity to an in-group is similar. As a court poet, Marot has a contract with power that permits him more freedom than the general public but still imposes restraint. Although his flippant comparison to the pope never would be permitted to a common person, it identifies Marot with the progressive court evangelists who were openly interested in religious reform and were often in a political struggle against the papacy. At the same time, the very absurdity of the argument protects Marot from too close an identification or too great a disagreement with any one religious party. Should the court eventually lean to Rome or Wittenberg, Marot, who neither affirms nor denies membership in any party, would remain safe.

## The Epistle to the King from Ferrara

The 1534 *affaire des placards,* however, changed historical circumstances to such an extent that Marot suddenly found his contract with power suspended. Whereas before he could be a religious progressive and still remain within the monarch's good graces, now the condemnation of the mass posted on the door of the king's bedroom rendered all adepts of religious reform suspect of treason and subject to the savage measures that ensued. Marot fled into exile. Epistles XXXIV–XLVII in Mayer's edition relate to this period. Marot's situation called up a new kind of poetry; he returns to the seriousness of his early days when he was first trying to win royal patronage. His conception of a formal epistle, however, is more mature. Rather than resort to Rhétoriqueur ornament, he maintains the clear conversational style he had developed in the epistles of the *Suite.* Only now, he at times speaks the religious discourse of a reformer or learnedly weaves in strains of Virgil and hints of the poetry that Ovid wrote to Augustus from exile.

The great epistle to Francis I is the best place to consider the echoes of both the Reformation and Ovid in Marot's poetry. It is the only poem of the group that goes beyond evangelistic commonplaces of the times. Marot issues a slippery denial of Lutheranism that raises scholarly eyebrows because he does not go so far as to condemn the Wittenberg reformer.[10] We, however, see Marot primarily concerned with re-establishing his contract with power. His refusal to condemn Luther comes more from his stance above religious parties than from his adherence to the German sect. His declaration of faith is far more moving here than in the epistle to Bouchard and "Hell," because we see him desperately trying to reaffirm previous relationships, identities, and political assumptions that belonged to a court situation that had vanished.

Marot's use of Ovid is also at its most interesting in the great epistle to Francis I. P. Villey has pointed out how Marot tried to modernize and Christianize Ovid in epistles Marot wrote to Marguerite and Francis I from Venice.[11] The great Ferrara epistle, however, contains no direct imitations but a radical rewriting of Ovid. The relationship is not one of imitation to predecessor but a more dialectical one usually referred to as intertextuality.[12]

**Summary.** The poem (*Epîtres,* XXXVI) up to line 120 is based on a hierarchy: judges, theologians, king, God. Marot first identifies himself with the king against Parisian judges (ll. 5–38). He points out that he has done nothing wrong except to read the poem "Hell"— with its denunciation of French justice—in front of the king, and he recalls that Francis I has saved him once before from the judges' unjust wrath. He then identifies himself with the king against the theologians of the Sorbonne (ll. 39–62). Their opposition to him comes from an ignorance that is ultimately against the king himself. They oppose the teaching of Greek, Latin, and Hebrew, which the king authorized in the Collège de France, as well as his entire cultural reform. Marot's condemnation of the Sorbonne gradually turns away from an identification with the king to one with God Himself in two sections that each culminate with a prayer. In the first (ll. 63–74), Marot says that the Sorbonne wants his execution, but prays that God may allow it if his death will save the lives of others. In the second (ll. 75–120), he brings up the accusation of Lutheranism. He was not baptized in the name of Luther but of Christ, he replies, and breaks into an eloquent prayer asking that his persecution result in a steadfast witness to the glory of God. Only in lines 121–22 does the poet return to earth: "Que dis-je? ou suis-je? O noble Roi Français,/Pardonne moi, car ailleurs je pensais" (What am I saying? where am I? O noble French king, / Pardon me, for I was elsewhere). This eloquent return not only communicates the poet's suffering but also establishes God at the top of the hierarchy because Marot has turned away from the king to pray.

In the second half of the poem (ll. 123–208), Marot launches into a narration of events that led to his present situation in Ferrara. Here he insists on his identity as a poet while he continues to maintain his loyalty to the king. He lashes out against the "sacrilegious" (l. 131) Judge Rhadamanthys who searched his house— "cabinet of the Holy Muses" (l. 134)—and found forbidden books. But he defends himself on the grounds of poetic license, (ll. 136–

42) and asserts that Christians have freedom to test the truth of all publications against the Bible (ll. 143–56). He says that he was going to court to deny any involvement in the "vile" *affaire des placards* when he was warned away and fled, fearing his prince (ll. 157–78). He stayed for a time with Marguerite (ll. 179–85), but when savage repression broke out that stupefied many a nation, he left "France, ingrate, ingratissime / A son Poète" (France, ungrateful, most ungrateful to her poet, ll. 192–93). Emphasizing his continued loyalty to the monarch, however, he says that he sought refuge with the king's cousin, Renée (ll. 197–208) and closes, briefly protesting his innocence (ll. 209–14).

**Analysis.**    The style of the poem reflects its heightened pathos without abandoning previous aesthetic ideals. Although maintaining a conversational plainness and clarity, Marot proceeds with an elevated, formal dignity as may be seen in the opening lines:

> Je pense bien que ta magnificence,
> Souverain Roi, croira que mon absence
> Vient par sentir la coulpe qui me point
> D'aucun méfait, mais ce n'est pas le point.
>
> (ll. 1–4)

(I am sure that your magnificence, / Sovereign King, will believe that my absence / Comes from feeling the guilt that goads me on / From some misdeed, but that is not the point.)

At times, however, Marot rises to great heights of passion, especially in the long prayer to God—an example of the preachy style—that ends with the apostrophe to Francis I of lines 121–22, cited above.

Marot's refutation is based on ad hominem arguments that reaffirm previously accepted identities rather than deal with concrete issues. The judges accuse him because they are hostile to his poem "Hell." The Sorbonne accuses him out of an ignorance that sets them against the king's cultural reform. He cannot be Lutheran because Luther is neither God the son nor God the father.

This last argument has been taken as a sign of Marot's Lutheranism because it rejects only the party name—as did Luther himself—but not the doctrine. Marot's use of Luther's own argument to distinguish himself from Luther is appropriate to his former situation

when, as a member of court above religious parties, he could approve
of aspects of Luther without being identified with him.

Marot's apostrophe to Francis I (ll. 121–22) that ends the long
prayer to God is surprisingly bold. The poet's admission that he
has turned his back on the king in order to pray recalls the higher
authority to which Francis himself must answer. Thus it probably
implies a warning against the king's excesses after the *affaire des
placards*. It is also a subtle intertextual allusion to Ovid's exile poetry.
Ovid often prays to Augustus as a god in the *Tristia*.[13] Marot,
however, never prays to the king. His opposition to Ovid is very
clear in the epistle addressed to Francis from Venice. There Marot
teaches his children to pray for the king, whereas Ovid in *Tristia*
II teaches his children to pray to Augustus.[14] Although the Ferrara
epistle contains no other allusions to Ovid, we consider Marot's
prayer a creative departure from Ovidian practice. It reminds Francis
that the king, unlike Caesar, is not a God. Such a reminder is
consistent with Marot's refusal to grant divine status to Luther earlier
in the poem. It also recalls the limits of poetic deification of royalty
that Marot practices in poems such as "L'Enfer." Francis may be a
new Augustus, but he is also a Christian king subject to God.

After having defined the judges and the Sorbonne in relation to
himself and the king and Luther in relation to himself and God,
Marot turns to affirm his own identity. As in "Hell," he emphasizes
his poetic calling:

> Bien est-il vrai que livres de défense
> On y trouva; mais cela n'est offense
> À un poète, à qui on doit lâcher
> La bride longue, & rien ne lui cacher,
> Soit d'art magique, nécromancie ou cabale;
> Et n'est doctrine écrite ne verbale
> Qu'un vrai Poète au chef ne dut avoir
> Pour faire bien d'écrire son devoir
> (ll. 135–42)

(Indeed it is true that they found / Forbidden books; but that is not an
offense / For a poet, to whom one must leave / A free rein, & from whom
one must hide nothing, / Be it magic, necromancy, cabbala; / And there
is no oral or written doctrine / That a true Poet should not have in mind
/ To carry out his duty to write well.)

Critical characterizations of Marot's attitude as that of an enlightened Christian or of a "free man," representative of an areligious concept of human dignity have been partial and limited. It is true that the appeal to the authority of the Bible (ll. 143–56) is an evangelistic theme. But Marot is more interested in establishing the right to poetic license than to freedom of thought in general. M. Screech, who recognizes the nature of this plea, however, does not allow Marot the freedom it so eloquently calls for; he obliges Marot's silences to be a declaration of Lutheranism instead of allowing him as a poet to remain open to all doctrines and ideas.[15]

Such a noncommittal position is at once courageous and poignant. Marot has not sold out to power. He openly denounces the savage repression in France and the shabby treatment he has received as a poet. He also calls Francis I to order, reminding him of his role as a Christian Augustus—a peaceful protector against the forces of ignorance and a guarantor of poetic freedom. The poignancy of Marot's arguments, however, comes from his blindness and alienation. His poem stands as a deluded attempt to turn back the clock to the pre-1534 court evangelism of a tolerant, enlightened Francis I and a previous contract with power, both of which were gone forever. Particularly touching is Marot's faith that the monarch is enlightened enough to read between the lines of the poem's silences and to be swayed by the logic of its arguments. The poem failed. Marot's silences condemned him. He was not to return to France without a solemn abjuration of his errors.

## Works of Doubtful Authenticity

These poems, all presumably written while Marot was in his last exile, are at times deeply moving. P. Jourda considers the poem "Le Riche en pauvreté" (The Rich Person despite Impoverishment, *O.L.,* Appendix 6) perhaps the best religious poem of the period. The "Balladin & dernier oeuvre de maître Clément Marot" (The Balladin and Last Work of Master Clement Marot, *O.L.,* Appendix 4) supposedly breaks off because the poet dies, pen in hand. In these poems Marot says all. Instead of the careful, complicated ironies of the earlier poems that shy away from doctrinal details, we have long, wordy expositions of articles of faith. Yet none of these poems goes further in religion than Marot's previous works except for the "Balladin," where the poet's allusion to the rebirth of the Christian church in Saxony is a clear affirmation of Lutheranism.

However, tempting as it appears, we do not believe that Marot wrote it or any other of these poems, not only because of the uncertain manuscripts and editions, but also for internal reasons. These poems bear an intertextual relationship to previous Marot poems that marks them as someone else's rewritings for purposes of doctrine. The "Sermon of the Good and Bad Pastor"[16] heavy-handedly resolves all the ambiguities of "The Deploration for Florimond Robertet." It develops the expression *vive foi* (living faith), which the "Deploration" only mentions, to show that it means "faith with works." Where the "Deploration" painted the portrait of a hideous death and then put words of self-praise in her mouth, the good pastor of the "Sermon" says that we should paint her as "beautiful and gracious" (l. 336). We believe with C.A. Mayer that Almanque Papillon wrote this poem. The "Complainte d'un Pastoreau Chrétien" (Complaint of a Christian Shepherd; *O.L.*, Appendix, 5) is as many have noticed a transparent transposition of the terms of the "Eclogue au Roi, sous les noms Pan & Robin." The "Rich Person despite Impoverishment" develops the same commonplace as the "Epistle to the Savoisien Sisters": suffering and poverty are better than delight and wealth because they are our participation in the crucifixion of our Master, Jesus Christ. The "Balladin" rewrites the contrast between Venus and Christine (i.e., Christianity) of the epistle that Marot wrote to Reneé of Ferrara from Venice (*Epîtres,* XLIII). Now we have a contrast between the physically plain but spiritually beautiful Christine and the outwardly dazzling but inwardly corrupt and wicked Simonne (the Roman church).

Furthermore, even though the "Balladin" is incomplete, the point at which it breaks off is too calculated to be true. The word *Balladin* refers to a kind of dance—the associations with a death dance are obvious in a poem that the title announces is the author's last poem. In the beginning of the poem, the author calls for an end to the dance so that he can tell the story of Christine and Simonne. The poet supposedly stops writing and dies at the time of his conversion when Christine invites him to learn her dance. During this dance, the wings of love transpose the poet to a beautiful forest and valley. The images of rebirth into paradise are clear (cf. the suckling bear, l. 293).

That Marot would die just at the moment he was writing about his spiritual rebirth is too calculated and cheaply transparent to be true. We believe this poem to be a forgery written by someone who wanted to prove that the poet was a Lutheran.

Marot's religion will always be something of a mystery to us. We cannot absolutely prove that this deathbed confession of the Lutheran faith did not come from him. However, in the remainder of his poetry, including his translation of the psalms, he always maintained a stance above religious parties and identified with the court evangelism of Marguerite and Briçonnet. We believe that his Lutheranism, if it did come, came only when he was pushed to the brink of the grave and had no hope of returning home.

# Chapter Twelve
# Conclusion

## Style and Genre

In returning to the 1538 edition, we realize that Marot worked out a system of genres and styles, most of which embody some form of the low style. Although Marot consistently tends toward a simplicity that suggests the spoken word, the division of his poetry into many genres—many kinds of simplicity—reveals the careful work of a writer. Most of Marot's epistles, epigrams, and epitaphs belong to what we have called the plain style. It is a type of low style that harks back to Martial and is noted for its realism, wit, and intellectuality. It reproduces the refined speech of a person at court, but it can at times descend to bawdiness.

The rondeau and some of the ballades are early examples of this plain-style manner. Although the medieval conventions make these genres seem highly ornamented to us, they must have seemed refreshing simplifications of old conventions in the Renaissance. Marot's plain style includes the style that Boileau referred to as *élégant badinage,* but there is much more arrogance in its nonchalant manner of plain speaking than Boileau's catch phrase would imply.

The songs belong to another kind of low style based on popular conventions. They have a simple, easy syntax like the plain style, but they lack the intellectuality and distance from feeling that we see in the plain-style genres.

Satire traditionally belongs to the realm of the plain style, but Marot stretches the conventions to their limits. The plain style implies a complicity between reader and audience. Marot's coqs-à-l'âne assume so much that they are incomprehensible except to the person for whom they were written. In "Hell," and some of the ballades, Marot ironically casts a plain-style perspective on more formal types of ornamentation. The result is poems that at first sight appear lofty but in fact make fun of loftiness.

The complaints and elegies represent an ornate yet flowing manner traditionally associated with the middle style. The complaints of the *Adolescence* are middle-style poems that scale down the formal Rhétoriqueur genre and reemphasize disconsolate mourning. "The Deploration for Florimond Robertet," on the other hand, remains a full-dress funeral piece in which low-style elements such as realistic details and intransigent mourning create an ironic distance from religious doctrines. The elegies embody a lower style than the complaints. They belong to a long tradition of European ornate low-style love lyric. They hark back to Ovid's *Amores* even though they are based on medieval *trouvère* conventions, for they are a French equivalent of the Roman poet's works. The death elegies are also in an ornamented low style. They are fables that deal with satirical subjects such as revenge, embezzlement, and marital jealousy.

The eclogues show us still other uses of the low style. They are courtly pastorals that use low-style conventions to discuss lofty subjects, or they play low style against high style for special effects.

The *chants divers* of the 1538 edition contain a special category of middle to high style poetry. Although some of the poems have satirical elements that downplay formality, they all have their points of departure in the upper reaches of the hierarchies of styles and subjects.

The presence of low-style elements throughout Marot's poetry relaxes decorum and gives Marot's poetic voice the nonchalance of Castiglione's courtier—a nonchalance that Marot abandoned when he was obliged to win new patronage. Yet it is this very nonchalance that is the source of so many different readings of Marot's poetry. Although one of its origins is an evangelical faith in a God that transcends all languages, it is also a signal of membership in an aristocratic elite whose position allowed it to take liberties with decorum. Yet at times these same liberties drove Marot away from the very society he wished to join. Unlike the romantic or modern poet who often assumes isolation and alienation as the very condition of poetry, Marot, until the end of his life, considered the court to be the only place in which his poetry could thrive. Such trust was neither naive nor sycophantic. Marot was proud to belong to such an elite and was very much aware that he owed his privileged position to his talent. Although much of his poetry is humble, as is appropriate when he speaks to persons of higher position, he can also be arrogant.

Marot was low in terms of the court hierarchy, but not in terms of the society at large. He treated the judges of Châtelet and the theologians of the Sorbonne contemptuously because he considered himself with the rest of the court above their laws and theological distinctions. As in many authoritarian regimes, he as a writer enjoyed greater freedom than commoner members of society. Still, he had to remain within certain limits. Those limits are not clear to us today. For example, in the great epistle to Francis I, which Marot wrote from Ferrara to protest his innocence, he stood up to Francis I and implied that because of the king's actions, France was guilty of having rejected her poet.

## A Court Religion

This perspective is especially important to understanding Marot's religion, which, with the exception of apocryphal poems written in exile, is always expressed in relation to a patron. Most often his religion is the court evangelism of Marguerite, Lefèvre d'Etaples, and Guillaume Briçonnet—a fluctuating belief in a time before the distinctions between Protestant and Catholic had hardened into rigid warring factions. His religious writing stood above religious parties and was open to all new ideas, but at heart it was nonschismatic. It is true that the French monarchy's relations with Rome were often strained throughout this period, but the king's policies had more to do with French territorial aspirations in Italy and a long-standing Gallican desire for autonomy in French church governance than with a desire to form a new church. When the chips were really down, the monarchy stood with Rome on church unity. Thus Marot's irreverence for the papacy was tolerable to the court as was his attack on justice. It was within these freedoms that he was allowed to be irreverent some of the time, but not necessarily all of the time.

There are occasions when Marot seems more extreme than his careful noninvolvement elsewhere suggests. For example, his voice is more impassioned and partisan in the poetry he wrote during the first exile to the Savoisien sisters, Renée of Ferrara and Marguerite. These poems, however, seem to have been written in order to gain much needed patronage at a difficult time when the *affaire des placards* had sent Francis I into a panic, and writers who had previously been within the limits accorded to the arts were suddenly on the wrong side. Furthermore, both Renée and Marguerite were members of the royal family. The court itself was split, and Marot had no choice but to address the factions that still supported him. Later, when he returned from exile, he toned down several of these poems in the 1538 manuscript he presented to Montmorency. During the second exile with Calvin, Marot was once again in search of a patron. On this occasion, however, despite similar pressures, he did not deviate from the court evangelism. He opened his translation of the psalms, which he dedicated to the council of Geneva, with an uncompromising alliance with tradition—his version of the Hail Mary. We do not call Marot's sincerity into question. the fact of the matter is that politics are inseparable from religion in most of Marot's poetry.

The only possible exceptions are the poems of doubtful authenticity. However, in stylistic terms, they are too overtly religious to be from his pen. In stylistic terms, they are quite different from Marot's previous poetry. Their wordiness marks them as probable forgeries which radical reformers wrote to fill in the gaps left by Marot's elliptical plain-style poems. If Marot did write them, and we find this implausible, they indicate a crisis so traumatic that it temporarily changed his style. They show Marot alienated and alone, turning to his God for comfort and solace. Yet this God is a God of the gap left by the absence of court support. Alongside these poems, which he may or may not have written, are a whole series of authentic poems from the last year of Marot's life that were part of his unrealistic yet concerted attempt to return to court. Faith in the court remained as essential to Marot as faith in God.

## Marot and Posterity

If Marot's nonchalance brought him glory and exile in turn, it also led to bizarre shifts in posterity's vision of him. He still remains the model for epigrams in French, and his plain style inspired La Fontaine's fables. Ronsard wrote constantly with Marot in mind. Spenser in England copied Marot's eclogues. However, as the French of Marot's writings became archaic, his plain style ironically led to lighter currents of manneristic poetry. The *précieux* poets of the seventeenth century found themselves in the virtuoso aspect of Marot's originally plain-speaking rondeaux. An eighteenth-century Marotic school believed that a few quaint archaisms were enough to imitate the poet's style.

Marot's poetic genius far transcends these lighter aspects of his influence and reputation. His ideal of imitation that connects with the roots of one's native language brings out new possibilities for the future. His dynamic use of the popular and natural elements in French offers a model of liberation from formal restraint. Such secrets for a living, unaffected poetry still have much to recommend them in the twentieth century.

# Notes and References

*Chapter One*

1. Material for Chapter One is drawn from several biographies of Marot. These overlap to such an extent that it is impossible to give precise notes. The main books used were P. A. Becker, *Clément Marot, sein Leben und seine Dichtung* (Munich, 1926); the G. Guiffrey biography that constitutes the first volume of his edition of Marot's *Oeuvres*, (Geneva, 1969); H. Guy, *Histoire de la poésie française au XVIe Siècle*, Tome II, *Clément Marot et son école* (Paris, 1968); P. Jourda, *Marot*, new ed. (Paris, 1967), pp. 5–58; C. A. Mayer, *Clément Marot* (Paris, 1972); J. Plattard, *Marot, sa carrière poétique, son oeuvre* (Geneva, 1972), pp. 7–89, and P. Villey *Marot et Rabelais* (Paris, 1967), pp. 1–153. Since the shortened titles of all these books is *Marot,* we shall refer to them hereafter by author and page number. Other important sources we referred to were Imbart de la Tour, *Les Origines de la réforme* (Paris: Hachette, 1905–1935), 4 vol., and A. Renaudet, *Préréforme et humanisme à Paris pendant les premières guerres d'Italie (1494–1517)*, 2d ed. (Paris, Librairie d'Argences, 1953). Also helpful for background on the psalms was M. Jeanneret's "Marot traducteur des Psaumes entre le Néo-platonisme et la Réforme," *Bibliothèque d'Humanisme et Renaissance* 27 (1965):629–43.

2. *Oeuvres lyriques,* LXXXIX, ed. C.A. Mayer (London, 1964). Hereafter cited in the text as *O.L.* Although we follow the order of the 1538 edition, we shall refer the reader to the modern Mayer edition. Other abbreviations cited in text are *Epîtres* (*Les Epîtres;* London, 1958); *O.D.* (*Oeuvres diverses;* London, 1966); *O.S.* (*Oeuvres satiriques;* London, 1962); *Epig.* (*Les Epigrammes;* London, 1970); and *T.* (*Les Traductions;* Geneva, 1980). All translations in this study are mine unless otherwise indicated. I have modernized the spelling in all French quotations.

3. *O.D.,* XXXI, LXXV, LXXVI; *Epîtres,* III, and Appendix I.

*Chapter Two*

1. See E. Faral, *Les Arts poétiques du XIIe et du XIIIe siecle* (Paris: Champion, 1971), pp. 86–87.

2. For more details, see W. Trimpi's *Ben Jonson's Poems: A Study of the Plain Style* (Stanford: Stanford University Press, 1962), and J. Houston, *The Rhetoric of Poetry in the Renaissance and Seventeenth Century* (Baton Rouge and London: Louisiana State University Press, 1983).

3. Guy, p. 113.

4. See J. Seznec, *Survival of the Pagan Gods,* trans. B.F. Sessions (New York: Bollingen, 1953), p. 12.

5. The most recent discussion of this may be found in Frances Yates's *Astraea* (London and Boston: Routledge & Kegan Paul, 1975), pp. 2–28.

6. Mayer, p. 29.

7. *La Concorde des deux langages,* ed. Frappier (Geneva: Droz, 1947).

8. Villey, p. 8.

9. Guy, p. 115; Jourda, p. 79; and Mayer, p. 32.

10. P. Leblanc, *La Poésie religieuse de Clément Marot* (Paris, 1955), p. 29; R. Griffin, *Clément Marot and the Inflections of Poetic Voice* (Berkeley, 1974), p. 119. Both works hereafter will be referred to by author and page only.

11. P.M. Smith, *Clément Marot* (London, 1970), p. 68. Hereafter referred to by author and page number.

12. See P. A. Becker, "Clement Marot und Lukian," *Neuphilologische Mitteilungen* 23 (1922):57–84.

13. For a discussion, see T. C. Burgess, *Epideictic Literature,* (Chicago: University of Chicago Press, 1902), pp. 89–261.

14. Beroaldus's "Carmen lugubre de dominicae passionis die" and Barthelemy de Loches's "Ennea ad sospitalem Christum," respectively.

15. R. Lebègue, "La Source d'un poème religieux de Marot," in *Mélanges offerts à Abel Lefranc.* (Geneva, 1972), pp. 58–74.

16. Guiffrey, 2:58.

*Chapter Three*

1. E. Langlois, *Recueil d'arts de seconde rhétorique* (Paris: Imprimerie nationale, 1902), p. 271.

2. T. Sebillet, *Art poétique* (Paris, 1932), p. 155.

3. P. Fabri, *Grand et vrai art de pleine rhétorique* (1889–90; reprint, Geneva: Slatkine, 1969), I:38–39 and I:194–207.

4. See Brunetto Latini, *Livre du Trésor* 3:16, as cited in J. J. Murphy, *Rhetoric in the Middle Ages: A History of Rhetorical Theory from St. Augustine to the Renaissance* (Berkeley, Los Angeles, and London: University of California Press, 1974), p. 231.

5. See H. Plattard, p. 141.

6. J. Vianey, *Les Epîtres de Marot* (Paris, 1935), pp. 39–41.

7. E. R. Curtius, *European Literature and the Latin Middle Ages,* tr. W. R. Trask (New York: Harper & Row, 1953), pp. 170–74.

8. *Sebillet, Art poétique,* p. 155.

9. Trimpi, *Ben Jonson,* pp. 142–43.

10. Vianey has observed as much. *Epîtres,* p. 46.

11. C. A. Mayer, *La Religion de Marot* (Paris, 1973), pp. 99–100.

12. See Pierre Jourda, *Marguerite d'Angoulême, duchesse d'Alençon, reine de Navarre* (Paris: Champion, 1930), 1:178–79; and Calvin's Letter to Daniel in A. L. Herminjard, *Correspondance des réformateurs dans les pays de langue française* (Niewkoop, 1965–66), 3:438, pp. 106–11.

13. M. A. Screech, *Marot évangélique* (Geneva, 1967), pp. 39–45. Hereafter referred to as Screech.

14. See G. Defaux, "Rhétorique, silence et liberté dans l'oeuvre de Marot: Essai d'explication d'un style," *Bibliothèque d'Humanisme et Renaissance* 46 (1984):321.

15. Vianey, p. 51.

## Chapter Four

1. For a more complete discussion, see O. B. Hardison, *The Enduring Monument* (Chapel Hill: University of North Carolina Press, 1962), pp. 113–18; and C. Martineau-Génieys, *Le Thème de la mort dans la poésie française* (Paris, 1978), pp. 326, 355.

2. Quintilian, *Institutio Oratoria,* tr. H. E. Butler, Loeb Classical Library, 12.10.58–60.

3. Plattard, pp. 112–13.

## Chapter Five

1. Sebillet, *Art poétique,* p. 131.
2. *O.D.,* pp. 139–72.
3. Sebillet, *Art poétique,* p. 132.
4. *O.D.,* pp. 67–135.
5. Sebillet, *Art poétique,* p. 120.
6. Ibid., p. 119.
7. *O.D.,* LXV.
8. *O.D.,* LXVI.
9. Trimpi, *Ben Jonson's Poems,* pp. 206–7.
10. T. Conley has given a new interpretation to one of Marot's most famous examples of antithesis. In the "Rondeau par contradictions" he sees a whole Freudian Oedipal scene that evokes a contrast between sacred and profane love in "A last spending of *Rhétorique:* A Reading of Marot's 'Par contradiction,' " *Esprit créateur* 18 (1978):82–91. In the rondeau "Hors du couvent" he finds suppressed allusions to money and gold. See Conley, "La Poétique du dehors: Autour d'un rondeau de Marot, XXXV, 'D'aucunes nonains,' " in *Poétiques, théorie et critique littéraire,* ed. F. Gray (Ann Arbor: University of Michigan, 1980), pp. 47–72. In the latter, it should be noted, Conley bases his interpretation of "Hors du couvent . . ." on spellings that exist only in the unreliable 1544 edition.

11. Mayer, introduction, *O.D.,* pp. 19–29.

12. See S. Minta, *Love Poetry in the Sixteenth Century* (Manchester, 1977), pp. 13–38, and the conventions that Roger Dragonetti lists for *trouvère* poetry of the twelfth- and thirteenth-centuries in *La Technique poétique des trouvères dans la chanson courtoise; contribution à l'étude de la rhétorique médiévale* (1960; reprint, Geneva: Slatkine, 1979).

13. See C. A. Mayer and D. Bentley-Cranch, "Clément Marot, poète pétarquiste," *Bibliothèque d'Humanisme et Renaissance* 28 (1966):32–51, and M. Cocco, *Tradizione cortese ed il Petrarchismo nella poesia di Clement Marot* (Florence, 1978).

14. The text and translation of Petrarch come from *Petrarch's Lyric Poems: The Rime Sparse and Other Lyrics,* trans. and ed. R. Durling (Cambridge: Harvard Unversity Press, 1976), pp. 94–95.

15. All alone is melancholy / Your Servant, who goes away from places / Where people want to sing, dance and laugh. / Alone in his bedroom, he wants to write about his tears / Because, when it rains, and the Sun of the Skies / Does not shine, every man worries, / And every Animal withdraws to its lair / All alone. / So now tears rain from my eyes. / And you who are my gracious Sun / Have left me in the shadow of martyrdom. / For these reasons I draw far away from others, / So not to weary them with my weariness, / All alone.

16. Alone and filled with care, I go measuring the most deserted / fields with steps delaying and slow, and I keep my eyes alert so / as to flee from where any human footprint marks the sand. / No other shield do I find to protect me from people's open / knowing, for in my bearing, in which all happiness is ex- / tinguished, anyone can read from without how I am aflame / within. / So that I believe by now that mountains and shores and rivers / and woods know the temper of my life, which is hidden from / other persons; / but still I cannot seek paths so harsh or so savage that Love does / not always come along discoursing with me and I with him. (trans. P. Durling).

17. See L. Keller, " 'Solo en pensoso,' 'Seul et pensif,' 'Solitaire et pensif,' mélancolie pétrarquienne et mélancolie pétrarquiste," *Studi francese* 49 (January–April 1973):3–14.

18. See Houston, *Rhetoric,* p. 8.

19. Mayer, by the way, refers to Petrarch's sonnet CLXXIII as a source for the sun imagery: "Mirando 'l sol de'begli occhi sereno" (Gazing at the clear sun of her lovely eyes, l. 1). But Marot here does not compare the lady's eyes to the sun.

20. Sebillet, *Art poétique,* p. 150.

21. V. L. Saulnier has effectively refuted J. Rollin's assertion that Marot himself was a musician. See J. Rollin, *Les Chansons de Clément Marot* (Paris, 1951), and Saulnier's review in *Bibliothèque d'Humanisme et Renaissance* 15 (1953):131–32.

22. *O.L.*, pp. 173–207.

23. Becker, pp. 226–27; and J. Rollin, *Les Chansons de Clément Marot*, pp. 79–82.

24. See his review of J. Rollin, p. 134.

25. Rollin, *Les Chansons de Clément Marot*, pp. 51–65.

*Chapter Six*

1. Sebillet, *Art poétique*, pp. 178–79.

2. See Smith, p. 82. In the later complaint, the dream that Marot has about Preudhomme and the prosopopeia of Marot's dead father are stock Rhétoriqueur devices. More specifically, the poem recalls Molinet's "Trône d'Honneur," and Crétin's "Déploration sur le trépas de feu Okergan." This archaism is perhaps a parody, according to C. Martineau-Génieys, intended smilingly to recall the departed's old-fashioned tastes. (See *Thème de la mort*, p. 512.) It may well be because of a parodic intent that Marot does not represent intransigent mourning.

3. Quintilian, *Inst. Orat.*, 12.10.59.

4. Martineau-Génieys, *Thème de la mort*, pp. 465–76.

5. See Screech, pp. 51–52.

6. See Mayer, *Religion*, p. 127.

7. Martineau-Génieys, *Thème de la mort*, pp. 474–77.

8. M. Richter, "L'Evangelismo di Clement Marot, Letture della 'Déploration de Florimond Robertet,' " *Bibliothèque d'Humanisme et Renaissance* 35 (1973):258.

9. For Virgil's practice, see R. Poggioli, *The Oaten Flute: Essays on Pastoral Poetry and the Pastoral Ideal* (Cambridge: Harvard University Press, 1975), p. 74–76.

10. E. Z. Lambert, *Placing Sorrow: A Study of the Pastoral Elegy Convention from Theocritus to Milton* (Chapel Hill, 1976), p. 111.

11. See Lambert, *Placing Sorrow*, pp. 107–12.

12. Poggioli, *Oaten Flute*, p. 74.

13. Leblanc, pp. 107–8.

14. *Oeuvres*, 4:356, n. 2. The complaint for Guillaume Preudhomme [*O.L.*, IX] also reduces the lament to a minimum. A poem of praise addressed to the departed's son, it seems to be intended to flatter a possible new patron, whom Marot desperately needed in 1543, rather than to console. Marot says at the end that the only recompense he wants is that the son emulate his father (ll. 153–56).

15. See Lambert, *Placing Sorrow*, p. 109.

16. Martineau-Génieys, *Thème de la mort*, p. 506.

17. For a very different but extremely penetrating reading of this poem, see L. Spitzer's "Zu Marots Eglogue au Roy soubs les noms de Pan et Robin." *Romanistisches Jahrbuch* 9 (1958):161–73.

*Chapter Seven*

1. See G. Joseph, "Rhetoric, Intertextuality, and Genre in Marot's *Elégies Déploratives,*" *Romanic Review* 72 (January 1981):25.
2. "Beautiful low style" in "À son livre," *Oeuvres complètes,* ed. P. Laumonier (Paris: Didier, 1959), 7:324, l. 174.
3. Houston, *Rhetoric,* p. 61.
4. Sebillet, *Art poétique,* p. 155.
5. Dragonetti, *Technique poétique des trouvères,* p. 307.
6. J. E. Clark, *Élégie: The Fortunes of a Classical Genre in Sixteenth-Century France,* (The Hague and Paris, 1975), p. 191.
7. Sebillet, *Art poétique,* p. 155.
8. C. Scollen, *The Birth of the Elegy in France, 1500–1550* (Geneva, 1967), pp. 13-14.
9. Sebillet, *Art poétique,* p. 155.
10. V. L. Saulnier, *Les Elégies de Clément Marot,* new ed. (Paris, 1968), pp. 52–64.
11. Ibid., pp. 105–10.
12. *O.D.* LXXXIII.
13. Fabri, *Rhétorique,* 1:38–39 and 199.
14. For a discussion of this technique, see Dragonetti, *Technique poétique des trouvères,* p. 294.
15. J. E. Clark calls this a "logical refrain" and gives several interesting examples in his *Élégie,* p. 31.
16. For a discussion of these topics, see Aphthonius's *Progymnasmata,* tr. Ray Nadeau, *Speech Monographs* 19 (1952):259.
17. For further details, see Joseph, "Rhetoric," pp. 22–24.
18. Martineau-Génieys, *Thème de la mort,* p. 497.

*Chapter Eight*

1. Villey, p. 40; Vianey, pp. 55–56; Guy, p. 150; Jourda, p. 116.
2. Plattard, p. 149 and Griffin, p. 78.
3. See Plattard, pp. 136–37.
4. Mayer, p. 217.
5. Sebillet, *Art Poétique,* pp. 167–68.
6. For a fuller discussion, see Mayer, pp. 212–18.
7. See C. E. Kinch, *La Poésie satirique de Clément Marot* (Paris, 1940), pp. 159–83.
8. See Plattard, p. 130.
9. Ibid., pp. 130–31.
10. See Villey, p. 93.
11. Vianey, p. 101.
12. Guy, p. 324.
13. Vianey, p. 96.

14. Mayer, p. 388.
15. Smith, pp. 238–41.
16. Sebillet, *Art poétique français,* p. 141.
17. Ibid., p. 136.
18. Houston, *Rhetoric,* pp. 87–89.
19. For a more detailed study of the prayers, see Leblanc, pp. 137–46.

*Chapter Nine*

1. E. Pasquier, *Recherches de la France* (Paris, 1633), 7:614.
2. Sebillet discusses only the necessary brevity of the epigram. See *Art poétique,* pp. 103–105.
3. Bibliothèque Nationale call number for the Dolet edition I consulted is Ye 1457–1460.
4. For a brilliant linguistic approach to this poem, see F. Rigolot's "Poétique et onomastique: L'épigramme de Semblançay," in *Poétique* 18 (1974):194–203.
5. See the articles "Sire" and "Monsieur" in R. Cotgrave's 1611 *Dictonarie of the French and English Tongues,* ed. W. S. Woods (Columbia: University of South Carolina Press, 1968).
6. J. Vianey, *Pétrarquisme en France au seizième siècle* (Montpelier, 1909), p. 49.
7. Villey, p. 63.
8. Petronius, "Me nive candenti," in *Anthologia Latina,* ed. F. Buecheler and A. Riese (Leipzig: Tuebner, 1906) 1.2., no. 706.
9. Griffin, *Marot,* p. 185.
10. C. A. Mayer and D. Bentley-Cranch, "Clément Marot, poète pétrarchiste," pp. 32–51.
11. "Iulia sola potes nostras extinguere flammas: / Non nive, non glacie, sed potes igne pari."
12. W. F. Panici includes a study of Marot's art of imitating Martial entitled "Domesticating a Form: Marot's *Epigrammes* and His Critics," in his forthcoming Yale doctoral dissertation.
13. *T.,* p. 114.
14. For a more detailed discussion see Houston, *Rhetoric,* pp. 5–8, 52.

*Chapter Ten*

1. E. Pasquier, *Recherches de la France,* 7:614. For G. Defaux, the psalm translations are the crowning spiritual and aesthetic achievement of Marot's poetic career. See "Silence et liberté," p. 320.
2. See O. Douen, *Clément Marot et le psautier huguenot* (Paris, 1878), 1:468–69.

3. P. Laumonier, *Ronsard, poète lyrique* (Paris: Hachette, 1909), pp. 17–21 and pp. 651–58; and P. Martinon, *Les Strophes* (Paris, 1911), pp. 1–38.

4. For a brief discussion of the thorny problems involved with the various editions of the psalms, see *T.*, pp. 44–49, 52–62.

5. See Leblanc, p. 311.

6. See, for example, J. L. Kugel, *The Idea of Biblical Poetry: Parallelism and its History* (New Haven and London: Yale University Press, 1981), pp. 159–64.

7. See M. Jeanneret, *Poésie et tradition biblique au xvie siècle: Recherches stylistiques sur les paraphrases des "Psaumes," de Marot à Malherbe* (Paris, 1969), pp. 165–86.

8. Cited in Douen, *Clément Marot et le Psautier Huguenot*, 1:471.

9. See J. Plattard, "Comment Marot entreprit et poursuivit la traduction des psaumes de David," *Revue des études rabelaisiennes* 10 (1912):352–55.

10. *T.*, pp. 342–44.

11. *The Writings-Kethubim: A New Translation of the Holy Scriptures according to the traditional Hebrew Text* (Philadelphia: Jewish Publication Society, 1982), pp. 9–10.

12. Jeanneret, *Tradition biblique,* p. 80.

13. Ibid., p. 59.

*Chapter Eleven*

1. Jourda, Screech, Leblanc, and Plattard have all discussed Marot's evangelism in this respect, and we see no need to repeat their arguments here.

2. Cited in Douen, *Psautier,* p. 472.

3. See Mayer, p. 124.

4. Plattard, p. 125.

5. For a description of Marot's style, but not in relation to generic hierarchies, see Jourda, pp. 136–37.

6. See, for example, Jourda, p. 137. Plattard, p. 124, comes to Marot's defense, however, in observing that the allegory only occasionally breaks through the realism of the poem.

7. For example, Plattard, p. 136.

8. Villey, p. 23, and Screech, p. 75, reach similar conclusions.

9. Jourda, p. 136. Marot's identification with king and court as above the law also presents an important qualification to Mayer's admiration of his courage (p. 126).

10. See, for example, Screech, pp. 16–20.

11. P. Villey, "À propos des Sources de deux epîtres de Marot," *Revue d'histoire littéraire de France* 26 (1919):235–38.

12. It also approaches Thomas Greene's "heuristic imitation." See *The Light in Troy* (New Haven and London: Yale University Press, 1982), pp. 40–43.

13. See *Tristia,* 2.53–54: "Per mare, per terras, per tertia numina . . ., per te praesentem conspicuumque deum."

14. See P. Villey, "À propos des Sources de deux épîtres de Marot," pp. 235–38.

15. Screech, p. 99.

16. *Oeuvres complètes de Clément Marot,* ed. B. St. Marc (Paris: Garnier, 1879), 1:66–76. Mayer does not include this poem in his edition.

# Selected Bibliography

## PRIMARY SOURCES

1. Important Renaissance editions of Marot's works

*Les Oeuvres de Clément Marot de Cahors, Valet de Chambre du Roi. Plus amples, & en meilleur ordre que paravant.* Edited by Constantin. Lyon: Rocher, 1544. Although Marot probably never saw this edition, it provided the format for most modern editions.

*Les Oeuvres de Clément Marot de Cahors, Valet de Chambre du Roi. Augmentées de deux livres d'epigrammes. Et d'un grand nombre d'autres oeuvres par ci devant non imprimées. Le tout soigneusement par lui même revu, et le mieux ordonné.* Edited by E. Dolet. Lyon: Dolet, 1538. Probably the last edition that Marot oversaw.

*Les Oeuvres de Clément Marot, Valet de Chambre du Roi, Desquelles le contenu s'ensuit. L'Adolescence clémentine. La Suite de l'adolescence, bien augmentées. Deux livres d'épigrammes. Le premier livre de la Métamorphose d'Ovide. Le tout par lui autrement et mieux ordonné que par ci devant.* Edited by Gryphius. Lyon: Gryphius, n.d. Virtually the same as the Dolet edition except for poems dedicated to Dolet which Marot removed.

2. Modern editions

*Oeuvres complètes de Clément Marot.* 2 vols. Edited by A. Grenier. Paris: Garnier, n.d. Still the only modern edition of the complete works in two volumes.

*Oeuvres de Clément Marot.* 5 vols. Edited by G. Guiffrey, J. Plattard, and R. Yve-Plessis. Geneva: Slatkine, 1969. Originally printed in 1911, this edition still has much to offer. Vol. 1 is a fine biography despite inaccuracies.

*Oeuvres poétiques.* Edited by Y. Guiraud. Paris: Garnier-Flammarion, 1973. A recent edition of Marot's works, but unfortunately not complete.

The following six volumes make up C. A. Mayer's edition of Marot's complete works. Mayer has reordered Marot's poems according to his own categories. Otherwise an excellent edition.

*Les Epîtres de Clément Marot.* London: Athlone, 1958.

*Oeuvres satiriques.* London: Athlone, 1962.

*Oeuvres lyriques.* London: Athlone, 1964.

*Oeuvres diverses.* London: Athlone, 1966.

*Les Epigrammes.* London: Athlone, 1970.
*Les Traductions.* Geneva: Slatkine, 1980.
*L'Adolescence clementine.* Edited by V. L. Saulnier. Paris: A. Colin, 1972.
A slightly inaccurate version of the first part of the 1538 edition.


SECONDARY SOURCES


1. Bibliography
Aulotte, R. "Quinze années d'études sur Clément Marot." *L'Information
Littéraire* 30 (1978):55–62. Most recent discussion of the present
state of Marot studies.
Mayer, C. A. *Bibliographie des oeuvres de Clément Marot. 1. Manuscrits. 2.
Editions.* Travaux d'Humanisme et Renaissance, nos. 10 and 13.
Geneva: Droz, 1954. Best bibliography of Marot's works to date.
———. "Les Oeuvres de Clément Marot: L'Economie de l'édition cri-
tique." *Bibliothèque d'Humanisme et Renaissance* 29 (1967):357–72;
hereafter referred to as *BHR.*
———. "Le Texte de Marot." *BHR* 14 (1952):314–28; 15 (1953):71–
91. A discussion of editions published in Marot's lifetime.
Saulnier, V. L. "Etat présent des études marotiques." *L'Information littéraire*
15 (1963):93–108. Precursor to Aulotte listed above. Still valuable.


2. Books and parts of books
Becker, P.A. *Clément Marot, sein leben und seine Dichtung.* Munich: Kellerer,
1926. One of the pioneer works in the field. Still valuable. Becker
studies Marot's works according to the first editions in which they
appear. His is the only other general study besides ours to be based
on editions published in Marot's lifetime.
Clark, J. E. *Elégie: The Fortunes of a Classical Genre in Sixteenth-Century
France.* The Hague and Paris: Mouton, 1975. Includes a good study
of Marot's elegies.
Cocco, M. *La Tradizione cortese et il petrarchismo nella poesia di Clément Marot.*
Florence: Olschki, 1978. The best study to date of the relation be-
tween Petrarchism and the medieval French courtly tradition in Mar-
ot's poetry.
Cooper, H. *Pastoral, Medieval into Renaissance.* Ipswich, Mass.: D. S. Brewer;
Totowa, N.J.: Rowman & Littlefield, 1977. Includes an interesting
section on Marot's eclogues.
Désiré, A. *Le Contrepoison des cinquante-deux chansons de Clément Marot.*
Edited by J. Pineaux. Geneva: Droz, 1977. A modern edition of
Désiré's attack on Marot's psalms.

**Douen, O.** *Clément Marot et le psautier Huguenot: Etude historique, littéraire et bibliographique.* 2 vol. Paris: Imprimerie Nationale, 1878. Still a classic despite inaccuracies and an attempt to make of Marot a Protestant.

**Gerhardt, M. I.** *Essai d'analyse littéraire de la pastorale dans les littératures italienne, espagnole, et française.* Te Assen Bij: Van Gorcum, 1950. A major study of the pastoral tradition in the Renaissance.

**Griffin, R.** *Clément Marot and the Inflections of Poetic Voice.* Berkeley, Los Angeles, and London: University of California Press, 1974. A fresh perspective on Marot's works, although sometimes difficult to follow.

**Guy, H.** *Histoire de la poésie française au xvie siècle.* Vol. 2, *Clément Marot et son école.* 1926. Reprint. Paris: Champion, 1968. Despite prejudices, still an insightful account.

**Hanisch, G.** *Love Elegies of the Renaissance: Marot, Louise Labé and Ronsard.* Saratoga: Anma Libri, 1979. Includes a general presentation of Marot's love elegies.

**Hulubei, A.** *L'Eglogue en France au seizième siècle.* 2 vol. Paris: Droz, 1938. Pioneer study of the French genre.

**Hutton, J.** *The Greek Anthology in France and in the Latin Writers of the Netherlands to the Year 1800.* Ithaca, N.Y.: Cornell University Press, 1946. Important pages on Marot's epigrams.

**Jeanneret, M.** *Poésie et tradition biblique au xvie siècle: Recherches stylistiques sur les paraphrases des "Psaumes," de Marot à Malherbe.* Paris: Corti, 1969. Fresh perspectives on Marot's psalm translations.

**Jourda, P.** *Marguerite d'Angoulême, duchesse d'Alençon, reine de Navarre.* Paris: Champion, 1930. Biography of this influential Renaissance woman who was Marot's first patron.

——. *Marot.* New ed. Paris: Hatier, 1967. A general study of Marot's works that is particularly good on matters of style.

**Kinch, C. E.** *L'Poésie satirique de Clément Marot.* Paris: Boivin, 1940. An old but at times still useful study of Marot's satire.

**Lambert, E. Z.** *Placing Sorrow: A Study of the Pastoral Elegy Conventions from Theocritus to Milton.* Chapel Hill: University of North Carolina Press, 1976. Fine pages on Marot's eclogue for Louise de Savoie.

**Laumonier, P.** *Ronsard, poète lyrique.* Paris: Hachette, 1909. One of the first to show the link between Marot's psalms and Ronsard's odes.

**Leblanc, P.** *La Poésie religieuse de Clément Marot.* Paris: Nizet, 1955. The first study on Marot's religion. Thorough and still valuable.

**Lerber, W. de.** *L'Influence de Clément Marot aux xviie et xviiie siècles.* Paris: Champion, 1920. Best study of Marot's reputation and influence in the seventeenth and eighteenth centuries.

**Martineau-Génieys, C.** *Le Thème de la mort dans la poésie française.* Paris: Champion, 1978. Fine pages on Marot and Briçonnet.

Martinon, P. *Les Strophes; Etude historique et critique sur les formes de la poésie en France depuis la Renaissance.* Paris: Champion, 1911. Shows that Marot is the father of modern French prosody.

Mayer, C. A. *Clément Marot.* Paris: Nizet, 1972. A fully documented study of Marot's life and works. Extensive use of archival materials.

———. *La Religion de Marot.* 1960. Reprint. Paris: Nizet, 1973. Sees Marot as interested in humanist, moralist concerns.

Minta, S. *Love Poetry in the Sixteenth Century.* Manchester: Manchester University Press, 1977. Sees little Petrarchan influence in Marot's poetry.

Pasquier, E. *Recherches de la France.* Paris: Toussaint Quinet, 1633. Considers Marot a great poet and every bit as good as Ronsard.

Plattard, J. *Marot, sa carrière poétique son oeuvre.* 1938. Reprint. Slatkine: Geneva, 1972. Still a useful presentation of Marot's life and works.

Rollin, J. *Les Chansons de Clément Marot.* Paris: Fischbacher, 1951. Best for location of musical settings to Marot's songs.

Saulnier, V. L. *Les Elégies de Clément Marot.* Paris: SEDES, 1968. A thorough study of the genre.

Scollen, C. M. *The Birth of the Elegy in France, 1500–1550.* Geneva: Droz, 1967. Suggests the influence of Ovid's *Heroides* on Marot.

Screech, M. A. *Marot évangélique.* Geneva: Droz, 1967. Marot is an evangelical Christian who had his Lutheran moments.

Sebillet, T. *Art poétique français.* Edited by F. Gaiffe. Paris: Droz, 1932. An "art of poetry" based largely on Marot's example.

Smith, P. M. *Clément Marot: Poet of the French Renaissance.* London: Athlone, 1970. A recent study of Marot's life and works.

Vianey, J. *Les Epîtres de Marot.* Paris: Société Française d'Editions Littéraires et Techniques, 1935. A thorough and often insightful study of Marot's epistles.

———. *Le Pétrarquisme en France au seizième siècle.* Montpelier, Coulet: 1909. Villey has refuted the Petrarchan influence Vianey finds in Marot.

Villey, P. *Marot et Rabelais.* 1923. Reprint. Paris: Champion, 1967. Still a very perceptive study of Marot's poetry. Chronological table of Marot's works included.

3. Articles

Becker, P. A. "Clément Marot und Lukian." Neuphilologische Mitteilungen. 23 (1922):57–84. Useful background for the "Judgment of Minos."

Conley, T. "A Last Spending of Rhétorique: A Reading of Marot's 'Par contradiction.' " *Esprit créateur* 18 (1978):82–91. This article is one of all too few studies that attempt a modern approach.

————. "La Poétique du dehors: Autour d'un rondeau de Marot, XXXV, 'D'Aucunes nonains.' " In *Poétique, théorie et critique littéraire*. Edited by F. Gray. Ann Arbor: University of Michigan, 1980. A study of Marot's rondeau that uses a modern critical approach.

Defaux, G. "Rhétorique, silence et liberté dans l'oeuvre de Marot: Explication d'un style." *BHR* 46 (1984):299–322. The first step in a forthcoming study of Marot in terms of J. Derrida's thoughts on logocentrism. We believe that Defaux concentrates too narrowly on Marot's religious faith to the exclusion of the worldlier political aspects of his poetry.

Françon, M. "Sur le premier sonnet français publié." *BHR* 33 (1971):365–66. An attempt to determine who wrote the first sonnet in French. Marot is a candidate.

Jeanneret, M. "Marot traducteur des psaumes entre le néo-platonisme et la réforme." *BHR* 27 (1965):629–43. Best account of the religious significance of Marot's psalm translations.

Joseph, G. "Rhetoric, Intertextuality, and Genre in Marot's *Elégies déploratives*." *Romanic Review* 72 (January 1981):13–25. A definition of Marot's death elegies in terms of rhetoric and intertextuality.

————. "Ronsard's Ode versus Marot's Epistle in Honor of François de Bourbon." *French Review* 54 (May 1981):788–96. A study of how Ronsard copies Marot's thought structures.

Katz, R.A. "The Lyricism of Clément Marot." *Kentucky Romance Quarterly* 19, Supp. 1 (1972):21–35. A perceptive study of Marot's lyricism.

Keller, L. "Solo e pensoso," 'Seul et pensif,' 'Solitaire et pensif,' mélancolie pétrarquienne et mélancolie pétrarquiste." *Studi francese* 49 (1973):3–14. A philological study linking Petrarch's *pensoso* with *mélancolie*.

Lebègue, R. "La Source d'un poème religieux de Marot." *Mélanges offerts à Abel Lefranc.*, pp. 50–74. 1936. Reprint. Geneva: Slatkine, 1972. A discussion of Marot's "Contemplative Prayer."

McClelland, J. "Sonnet ou quatorzain? Marot et le choix d'une forme poétique." *Revue d'histoire littéraire* 73 (1973):591–607. A contribution to the discussion of who wrote the first sonnet.

Mayer, C. A. "Du nouveau sur le sonnet français." *Studi Francese* 60 (1976):422–29. Another discussion of whether Marot wrote the first sonnet.

Mayer, C. A., and Bentley-Cranch, D. "Clément Marot poète pétrarquiste." *BHR* 28 (1966):32–51. Close study of Petrarchan influence, mainly in the rondeaux.

Plattard, J. "Comment Marot entreprit et poursuivit la traduction des psaumes de David." *Revue des études Rabelaisiennes* 10 (1912):321–355. Insightful.

Prescott, A. L. "The reputation of Clément Marot in Renaissance England." *Studies in the Renaissance* 18 (1971):173–202. Marot's influence in England.

Richter, M. "L'Evangelismo di Clément Marot, Lettura della 'Déploration de Florimond Robertet.' " *BHR* 35 (1973):247–258. A new look at Marot's great poem.

Rigolot, F. "Poétique et onomastique: L'épigramme de Semblançay." *Poétique* 18 (1974):194–203. A very perceptive account of the ambiguities in Marot's famous epigram.

Spitzer, L. "Zu Marots 'Eglogue au Roy soubs les noms de Pan et Robin'." *Romanistisches Jahrbuch* 9 (195):161–73. One of the best articles ever written on Marot.

Tomarken, A. "Clément Marot and the *Grands Rhétoriqueurs.*" *Symposium* 32 (1978):41–55. Interesting study of the little epistle to the king.

Villey, P. "Marot et le premier sonnet Français." *Revue d'histoire littéraire de France* 27 (1920):538–47. Still another article in the discussion of who wrote the first sonnet in French.

Villey, P. "A propos des Sources de deux epîtres de Marot." *Revue d'histoire littéraire de France* 26 (1919):220–45. Study of Ovid's influence on Marot's epistles written in exile.

# Index